# HYBRID CARS: INCREASING FUEL EFFICIENCY AND REDUCING OIL DEPENDENCE

## United States Congress House of Representatives Committee on Government Reform, Subcommittee on Energy and Resources

The BiblioGov Project is an effort to expand awareness of the public documents and records of the U.S. Government via print publications. In broadening the public understanding of government and its work, an enlightened democracy can grow and prosper. Ranging from historic Congressional Bills to the most recent Budget of the United States Government, the BiblioGov Project spans a wealth of government information. These works are now made available through an environmentally friendly, print-on-demand basis, using only what is necessary to meet the required demands of an interested public. We invite you to learn of the records of the U.S. Government, heightening the knowledge and debate that can lead from such publications.

Included are the following Collections:

Budget of The United States Government
Presidential Documents
United States Code
Education Reports from ERIC
GAO Reports
History of Bills
House Rules and Manual
Public and Private Laws

Code of Federal Regulations
Congressional Documents
Economic Indicators
Federal Register
Government Manuals
House Journal
Privacy act Issuances
Statutes at Large

# HYBRID CARS: INCREASING FUEL EFFICIENCY AND REDUCING OIL DEPENDENCE

# HEARING

BEFORE THE

## SUBCOMMITTEE ON ENERGY AND RESOURCES

OF THE

## COMMITTEE ON GOVERNMENT REFORM

## HOUSE OF REPRESENTATIVES

ONE HUNDRED NINTH CONGRESS

SECOND SESSION

JULY 20, 2006

## Serial No. 109–233

Printed for the use of the Committee on Government Reform

Available via the World Wide Web: http://www.gpoaccess.gov/congress/index.html
http://www.house.gov/reform

U.S. GOVERNMENT PRINTING OFFICE

34–660 PDF          WASHINGTON : 2007

For sale by the Superintendent of Documents, U.S. Government Printing Office
Internet: bookstore.gpo.gov   Phone: toll free (866) 512–1800; DC area (202) 512–1800
Fax: (202) 512–2250   Mail: Stop SSOP, Washington, DC 20402–0001

## COMMITTEE ON GOVERNMENT REFORM

TOM DAVIS, Virginia, *Chairman*

CHRISTOPHER SHAYS, Connecticut
DAN BURTON, Indiana
ILEANA ROS-LEHTINEN, Florida
JOHN M. McHUGH, New York
JOHN L. MICA, Florida
GIL GUTKNECHT, Minnesota
MARK E. SOUDER, Indiana
STEVEN C. LaTOURETTE, Ohio
TODD RUSSELL PLATTS, Pennsylvania
CHRIS CANNON, Utah
JOHN J. DUNCAN, JR., Tennessee
CANDICE S. MILLER, Michigan
MICHAEL R. TURNER, Ohio
DARRELL E. ISSA, California
JON C. PORTER, Nevada
KENNY MARCHANT, Texas
LYNN A. WESTMORELAND, Georgia
PATRICK T. McHENRY, North Carolina
CHARLES W. DENT, Pennsylvania
VIRGINIA FOXX, North Carolina
JEAN SCHMIDT, Ohio
BRIAN P. BILBRAY, California

HENRY A. WAXMAN, California
TOM LANTOS, California
MAJOR R. OWENS, New York
EDOLPHUS TOWNS, New York
PAUL E. KANJORSKI, Pennsylvania
CAROLYN B. MALONEY, New York
ELIJAH E. CUMMINGS, Maryland
DENNIS J. KUCINICH, Ohio
DANNY K. DAVIS, Illinois
WM. LACY CLAY, Missouri
DIANE E. WATSON, California
STEPHEN F. LYNCH, Massachusetts
CHRIS VAN HOLLEN, Maryland
LINDA T. SANCHEZ, California
C.A. DUTCH RUPPERSBERGER, Maryland
BRIAN HIGGINS, New York
ELEANOR HOLMES NORTON, District of
 Columbia
 ———
BERNARD SANDERS, Vermont
 (Independent)

DAVID MARIN, *Staff Director*
LAWRENCE HALLORAN, *Deputy Staff Director*
TERESA AUSTIN, *Chief Clerk*
PHIL BARNETT, *Minority Chief of Staff/Chief Counsel*

### SUBCOMMITTEE ON ENERGY AND RESOURCES

DARRELL E. ISSA, California, *Chairman*

LYNN A. WESTMORELAND, Georgia
JOHN M. McHUGH, New York
PATRICK T. McHENRY, NORTH CAROLINA
KENNY MARCHANT, Texas
BRIAN P. BILBRAY, California

DIANE E. WATSON, California
BRIAN HIGGINS, New York
TOM LANTOS, California
DENNIS J. KUCINICH, Ohio

### EX OFFICIO

TOM DAVIS, Virginia

HENRY A. WAXMAN, California

LAWRENCE J. BRADY, *Staff Director*
DAVE SOLAN, *Professional Staff Member*
LORI GAVAGHAN, *Clerk*
SHAUN GARRISON, *Minority Professional Staff Member*

# CONTENTS

# HYBRID CARS: INCREASING FUEL EFFICIENCY AND REDUCING OIL DEPENDENCE

## THURSDAY, JULY 20, 2006

House of Representatives,
Subcommittee on Energy and Resources,
Committee on Government Reform,
*Washington, DC.*

The subcommittee met, pursuant to notice, at 2:05 p.m., in room 2247, Rayburn House Office Building, Hon. Darrell E. Issa (chairman of the subcommittee) presiding.

Present: Representatives Issa and Watson.

Staff present: Larry Brady, staff director; Dave Solan and Ray Robbins, professional staff members; Joe Thompson, GAO detailee; Shaun Garrison, minority professional staff member; and Cecelia Morton, minority office manager.

Mr. Issa. In the essence of trying to minimize the waste of your time, I will ask unanimous consent that we begin without our reporting quorum. Without objection, so ordered.

I will do my opening statement and then, hopefully, the ranking member will be here by then. If not, we will make other provisions.

Good afternoon. I want to welcome everyone to this subcommittee hearing.

Today's record oil and gasoline prices underscore our country's need for more fuel-efficient automobiles. We need to use fuel more efficiently to lessen the dependence on imported oil from unstable areas of the world. Almost 70 percent of the oil consumed in the United States is used by the transportation sector. Therefore, to improve the Nation's energy security, it is vital that we increase fuel efficiency of the cars and trucks—particularly light trucks and SUVs—that we drive.

One of the more practical solutions in the near term and I might say in the present term is to increase the number of the hybrid vehicles on our Nation's roads. A hybrid is a vehicle that combines an electric motor and a battery pack with an internal combustion engine to increase fuel efficiency over traditional automobiles.

These one-time improvements have their limits. Today, we will explore these limits and how we can further advance in the future. Is the recapture of kinetic energy in its infancy, its midlife, or have we, in fact, gotten most of what we can get from this technology? Can we increase the efficiency of recapturing this energy into batteries or even capacitors? Additionally, hybrids have a reputation for superlow emissions. Can we accomplish more in the way of reductions of emissions using constant speed engines and the other attributes that often come with hybrid technology?

(1)

Currently, hybrids are about 30 percent more fuel efficient than nonhybrid counterparts, so they burn less fuel and emit fewer pollutants per mile travel than non-hybrid vehicles. Advances in hybrid technologies could potentially increase these benefits.

A complex series of factors influences an individual's decision to purchase a hybrid vehicle, including purchase price, cost of gasoline, government incentives and personal convictions. This is the brag part of it. As the owner of two hybrid vehicles and the previous owner of two other hybrid vehicles, I am convinced of their benefits, but I am also concerned about the low level of market penetration that limit the overall impact of hybrids on fuel efficiency of the U.S. fleet.

In an effort to better understand these competing factors, today's hearing on hybrid vehicles will focus on, but not be limited to, potential fuel efficiency and environmental benefits, cost-effectiveness, market penetration, government incentives, U.S. manufacturing capacity, and anticipated advances in technology.

[The prepared statement of Hon. Darrell E. Issa follows:]

**COMMITTEE ON GOVERNMENT REFORM**
**SUBCOMMITTEE ON ENERGY AND RESOURCES**

*OPENING STATEMENT OF*
*CHAIRMAN DARRELL ISSA*

Oversight Hearing:

**"Hybrid Cars: Increasing Fuel Efficiency and**
**Reducing Oil Dependence"**
*July 20, 2006*

Good afternoon everyone and welcome to our Subcommittee hearing.

Today's record oil and gasoline prices underscore our country's need for more fuel efficient automobiles. We need to use fuel more efficiently to lessen our dependence on imported oil from unstable areas of the world. Almost 70 percent of the oil consumed in the U.S. is used by the transportation sector. Therefore, to improve this nation's energy security, it is vital to increase the fuel efficiency of the cars we drive.

One of the more practical solutions for the near-term is to increase the number of hybrid vehicles on the nation's roads. A hybrid is a vehicle that combines an electric motor and battery pack with an internal combustion engine to increase fuel efficiency over that of traditional vehicles.

Although it is recognized that these improvements have their limits, today we will explore these limits and how we can advance further. Is the recapture of kinetic energy in its infancy? Can we increase the efficiency of recapturing this energy into batteries or even capacitors? Additionally, hybrids have the reputation for super low emissions. Can we accomplish more?

Currently, hybrids are about 30 percent more fuel efficient than non-hybrid vehicles, so they burn less fuel and emit fewer pollutants per mile traveled than non-hybrid vehicles. Advances in hybrid technologies could potentially increase these benefits.

A complex series of factors influences an individual decision to purchase a hybrid vehicle, including the purchase cost, gasoline cost savings, government incentives, and personal convictions. As an owner of two hybrid vehicles, I am convinced of their benefits, but am also concerned about the low levels of market penetration that limit the overall impact of hybrids on the fuel efficiency of the U.S. fleet.

In an effort to better understand these competing factors, today's hearing on hybrid vehicles will focus on: potential fuel efficiency and environmental benefits, cost-effectiveness, market penetration, government incentives, U.S. manufacturing capacity, and anticipated advances in hybrid technology.

We are privileged to have here today:

Dr. Andrew Frank
Director, University of California-Davis Hybrid Electric Research Center

Mr. David Hermance
Executive Engineer, Toyota Motor North America

Mr. John German
Manager, Environmental and Energy Analyses, American Honda Motor Company; and

Don MacKenzie
Vehicles Engineer, Union of Concerned Scientists.

I look forward to hearing from our witnesses.

**COMMITTEE ON GOVERNMENT REFORM**

*Subcommittee on Energy and Resources*
*DARRELL ISSA, CHAIRMAN*

Oversight Hearing:

**"Hybrid Cars: Increasing Fuel Efficiency and Reducing Oil Dependence"**

---

*BRIEFING MEMORANDUM*
**July 20, 2006, 2:00pm**
**Rayburn House Office Building**
**Room 2247**

**Summary**

Record oil and gasoline prices are magnifying the need for more fuel efficient automobiles. U.S. dependence on imported oil from unstable areas of the world and reliance on the hurricane-prone Gulf of Mexico region for refined petroleum products has reinforced the need to use fuels more efficiently. Almost 70 percent of oil consumed in the U.S. is used by the transportation sector.

Several technologies can help increase the fuel efficiency of the American auto fleet, and therefore increase energy security by reducing U.S. dependence on imported oil. Such technologies include bio-diesel fuel, hydrogen, ethanol, electric vehicles, and hybrid electric vehicles. However, many of these technologies are not yet cost effective or widely available. Increasing the number of hybrid electric vehicles on the road is one practical way to increase the fuel efficiency of the U.S. fleet in the near-term.

**Types of Hybrid Electric Vehicles**

Hybrid Electric Vehicles (HEVs, or hybrids) combine an electric motor and battery pack with an internal combustion engine. Hybrids are generally classified as (1) full hybrid, (2) mild hybrid, or (3) plug-in hybrid. A full hybrid is a vehicle that can move forward at low speeds without consuming any gasoline, such as a Toyota Prius or Ford Escape. Mild hybrids, like the Honda Civic, are vehicles that move from a standstill only if the internal combustion engine is engaged. Mild hybrids use the electric motor primarily to assist the gas engine when extra power is needed. Mild hybrids are further classified into the following subcategories:

- Stop/Start hybrid - This system shuts the internal combustion engine off and uses electricity from a battery when it would otherwise idle. The engine re-starts instantly on demand.

- Integrated Starter Alternator with Damping (ISAD) – This hybrid system allows the electric motor to help move the vehicle in addition to providing stop/start capability.

- Integrated Motor Assist (IMA) – The IMA hybrid system is similar to the ISAD but has a larger electric motor that provides more electricity that can be used to help move the vehicle.

Both full and mild hybrids require use of the gasoline internal combustion engine when reaching speeds greater than 20-25 mph.

Plug-in hybrid vehicles give the owner the option to charge the electric batteries using residential electric outlets. Plug-in hybrids have a larger electric battery system that allows the vehicle, once fully charged, to operate like a fully electric vehicle. Under 34 miles per hour (mph), the electric motor effectively powers the vehicle. Over 34 mph and during bursts of acceleration, the gasoline motor begins to help incrementally. When the electricity stored in the battery runs out, the gasoline engine starts and the plug-in hybrid vehicle operates like a regular hybrid.

**Hybrid Electric Vehicle Market**

Hybrids accounted for 1.2 percent of the total vehicles sold in model year 2005. However, the hybrid market has grown from two models and fewer than 10,000 vehicles sold in 2000 to 11 models and an estimated 212,000 vehicles sold in 2005. Furthermore, U.S. hybrid sales volumes are anticipated to grow by 268% between 2005 and 2012, according to the most recent update of the J.D. Power and Associates Automotive Forecasting Services Hybrid-Electric Vehicle Outlook.

Although hybrid cars have the potential to greatly increase the overall fuel efficiency of the nation's automobile fleet, the lack of hybrid vehicle production in the U.S. is a concern. Currently, Toyota is the hybrid market leader with 63.3 percent of the U.S. market, followed by Honda with 25 percent and Ford with 9.4 percent. Notably, Ford operates one of the few hybrid manufacturing facilities in the U.S. in Kansas City, Missouri. As illustrated in Table 1 below, American hybrid production greatly trails Japanese production in both the number of models and quantity.

**Table 1: Availability and Sales of Hybrid Electric Vehicles in the U.S.**
**(1st Quarter 2006)**

| BRAND | AVAILABLE | ORIGIN | HYBRID SALES (1st Qtr 2006) |
|---|---|---|---|
| Toyota Prius | NOW | Japan | 22,123 |
| Toyota Highlander | NOW | Japan | 7,881 |
| Honda Civic | NOW | Japan | 7,177 |
| Lexus RX 400h | NOW | Japan | 5750 |
| Ford Escape | NOW | U.S.A. | 4068 |
| Honda Accord | NOW | Japan | 1715 |
| Honda Insight | NOW | Japan | 210 |
| Mercury Mariner | NOW | U.S.A. | 205 |
| Honda Fit | NOW | Japan | N/A |
| GM Silverado | NOW | U.S.A. | N/A |
| GM Sierra | NOW | U.S.A. | N/A |
| Nissan Altima | Late 2006 | Japan | N/A |
| Toyota Camry | Late 2006 | Japan | N/A |
| Lexus GS | Late 2006 | Japan | N/A |
| Saturn VUE | Late 2006 | U.S.A. | N/A |
| Dodge Ram | Late 2006 | U.S.A. | N/A |
| Dodge Durango | 2007 | U.S.A. | N/A |
| Toyota Sienna | 2007 | Japan | N/A |
| Chevrolet Malibu | 2007 | U.S.A. | N/A |
| Porsche Cayenne | 2008 | Germany | N/A |

Source: http://www.hybridcars.com

**Benefits of Hybrid Electric Vehicles**

Fuel Efficiency and Potential Cost Savings

Hybrids are, on average, about 30 percent more fuel efficient than traditional internal combustion gasoline engines, so fuel costs are significantly lower with hybrids than with conventional vehicles. While hybrids generally cost several thousand dollars more than comparable conventional vehicles, the higher price is offset to some degree by lower fuel costs and tax incentives, discussed in more detail below. The combination of fuel cost savings and tax incentives allows buyers of certain hybrid vehicles to recover the price premium. Buyers of two hybrid vehicle models (Toyota Prius and Honda Civic Hybrid) are currently able to recover the price premium of buying the automobile with fuel cost savings and tax incentives. See Table 2, below for a cost comparison of model year 2006 conventional and hybrid Honda Civic automobiles.

**Table 2: Cost Difference for Hybrid (MY06) and Conventional (MY06) Honda Civic Sedan LX with automatic**

| | Cost in dollars |
|---|---|
| Hybrid purchase cost (MSRP) | 22,150 |
| Fuel cost savings | (4,300) |
| Federal tax credit (est.) | (2,100) |
| Hybrid net cost | 15,750 |
| Conventional purchase (MSRP) | 17,510 |
| Net cost difference | (1,760)[1] |

Source: Congressional Research Service

Further, converting a Toyota Prius or similar hybrid to a plug-in hybrid will increase its gasoline efficiency from nearly 50 miles per gallon (mpg) to 99 mpg, increasing fuel cost savings. However, the cost of converting vehicles from standard hybrid to plug-in hybrid is currently prohibitive at around $10,000-$12,000.

Reduced Dependence on Imported Oil

According to HybridCars.com, by the end of 2006 there will be nearly 700,000 hybrids on American roads. This represents approximately one-third of one percent of the 230 million vehicles in use. Given current trends of miles per person traveled, hybrids will save approximately 0.07 percent of fuel used by Americans—or nearly 100 million gallons in 2006. By the end of the decade, if current trends are maintained, there will be nearly 2 million hybrids on American roads. The total number of vehicles in the U.S. fleet is expected to grow from 230 million in 2006 to 250 million in 2010. Therefore, hybrids will have grown from 0.03 percent of vehicles in use in 2006 to 0.08 percent in 2010—with fuel savings of 300 billion gallons in 2010 or 0.2 percent of all fuel used by Americans.[2]

Given current trends in terms of vehicles in use and miles driven, as well as flat fuel economy trends for conventional and hybrid vehicles, fuel savings from the introduction of hybrids will reach 1 percent of all fuel used—over 2 trillion gallons—in about 20 years. At that point, Americans are expected to consume 80 trillion more gallons of gas than they do today. If these projections hold, hybrids will reduce the increasing rate of consumption rather than actually reducing (or even maintaining) today's rate of consumption. Most auto sales forecasters expect new hybrid sales to remain in the single digit percentage points for the next two decades. If hybrids could reach 10 percent penetration by 2010—requiring an aggressive increase in production and sales—then hybrid fuel savings would only then stem the growth in consumption and represent an effective measure for real reductions in gasoline usage.

---

[1] Based on $2.78 per gallon of gasoline; ten year life; 15,000 miles per year; not discounted over time.
[2] Bradley Berman at HybridCars.com is the source of information found in the "Reduced Dependence on Imported Oil" section of this briefing memo. HybridCars.com based its estimates, in part, on information obtained from Dr. Walter McManus at the University of Michigan Transportation Research Institute.

<u>Emission Reductions</u>

Hybrid cars also reduce air emissions because they replace less efficient vehicles in the U.S. fleet. Based on market share and fuel consumption data used in the previous section, hybrid cars account for substantial reductions in emissions of greenhouse gases (primarily carbon dioxide) and air toxics such as benzene in comparison to non-hybrid internal combustion vehicles. For example, in 2006, hybrid cars are estimated to emit about 850,000 fewer tons of carbon dioxide and about 4,500 fewer tons of benzene than the same number of non-hybrid cars would have emitted. By 2010, hybrids would account for estimated reductions of over 2 million tons of carbon dioxide and about 11,000 tons of benzene, and by 2020 reductions are estimated to rise to over 8 million tons of carbon dioxide and about 49,000 tons of benzene.[3]

<u>Use of Existing Infrastructure</u>

An attractive feature of hybrids is that no new fueling infrastructure is needed, since these vehicles are fueled by gasoline or diesel. This allows hybrid owners to purchase and operate their vehicles anywhere in the country, and long-distance travel is not limited by the fueling infrastructure.

<u>Other Benefits</u>

Other benefits of owning a hybrid vary in different states. In certain states, hybrids are allowed to use the High Occupancy Vehicle (HOV) lanes regardless of the number of passengers. In addition, hybrid owners in certain Californian cities may park without depositing coins at on-and- off metered parking spaces.

**Federal and State Government Hybrid Electric Vehicle Tax Incentives**

<u>Federal Incentives</u>

The Energy Policy Act of 2005 created the Alternate Motor Vehicle Tax Credit to encourage the purchase of hybrid vehicles. This credit took effect on January 1, 2006. For most hybrid car buyers, the new credits are more valuable than the prior incentives, which were a reduction of taxable income.[4] In order to qualify for the Alternate Motor Vehicle Tax Credit a consumer must:

- Purchase and take delivery of a qualifying vehicle on or after January 1, 2006.

---

[3] Subcommittee staff used data provided by HybridCars.com and the University of Michigan Transportation Research Institute and carbon dioxide and benzene emission factors from EPA (available at: http://www.epa.gov/oms/climate/420f05004.htm, and http://www.epa.gov/OMS/toxics.htm, respectively), to calculate emission reduction estimates.
[4] The previous tax deduction (eliminated in 2005) was more valuable for taxpayers who must pay the Alternative Minimum Tax or take a lot of deductions.

- Purchase the vehicle new, not used.

- Purchase the vehicle with the intent of using it, not reselling it.

The primary limitation of the credit is that the full amount only applies to the first 60,000 hybrids per carmaker, based on the quantity of hybrid vehicles manufactured and delivered to dealerships, rather than the number of hybrids sold. After the manufacturer hits that mark for a particular hybrid, the credit for that vehicle phases out over a 15-month period. The timing of the phase-out and amount of the credit during the phase-out period is unclear. According to Toyota, "the reductions may begin to apply as early as June 30, 2006 or September 30, 2006."[5] Specific details of the Alternate Motor Vehicle Tax Credit include:

- The credit will reduce your regular income tax liability, but not below zero.

- If you are eligible for multiple tax credits, the hybrid tax credit is taken last after all the other credits (e.g., child care tax credit, mortgage credit, and retirement savings credit) have been taken. Any tax liability left over by these reductions will be the maximum dollar limit of your hybrid tax credit. If your hybrid tax credit exceeds your maximum dollar limit, the excess is not refundable, and is lost forever.

- The excess cannot be carried over to another year, or given away to another person.

- The credit will not reduce your alternative minimum tax, if that applies to you. As stated in Toyota's statement about the new tax credits: "The benefit of the hybrid vehicle tax credit will also be substantially reduced or eliminated if the individual purchaser is subject to the federal alternative minimum tax."[6]

State Incentives

Currently, 23 States and the District of Columbia offer incentives to purchase hybrids. These incentives range from exempting hybrids from excise taxes to sales tax credits. See Appendix A on pages 7-12 for incentives offered by states and the District of Columbia for hybrid vehicle purchases.

---

[5] From: http://www.hybridcars.com/tax-deductions-credits.html
[6] From: http://hybridcars.com/tax.deductions-credits.html

## Hearing Focus

This hearing will assess the potential for hybrid vehicles to increase the overall fuel efficiency of the U.S. fleet and lessen the nation's dependence on imported oil, paying particular attention to issues regarding cost-effectiveness, market penetration, incentives, U.S. manufacturing capacity, and environmental benefits. This hearing will address the following questions:

- What are the potential benefits, in terms of fuel consumption and emission reductions, of increasing the number of hybrid vehicles in the U.S. fleet?

- What advances in hybrid technology are expected and by when?

- What is the projected market share for hybrids in the short and long term?

- Will hybrid technology become more cost competitive in comparison to conventional internal combustion technology?

- Why has the US auto industry lagged in developing hybrid cars?

- What further actions can Federal and state governments take to encourage consumers to purchase hybrid vehicles?

### Witnesses:

- **Dr. Andrew Frank**
  Director, University of California-Davis Hybrid Electric Research Center

- **Mr. David Hermance**
  Executive Engineer, Toyota Motor North America

- **Mr. John German**
  Manager, Environmental and Energy Analyses, American Honda Motor Company

- **Don MacKenzie**
  Vehicles Engineer, Union of Concerned Scientists

### STAFF CONTACT

Larry Brady, Staff Director
Subcommittee on Energy and Resources
B-349C Rayburn House Office Building

12

202.225.6427 / 202.225.2392 fax

## Appendix A
## Incentives Offered by States and the District of Columbia
## for Hybrid Vehicle Purchases[7]

**Arizona**: As of Jul. 9, Arizona Revised Statutes from the 47th session Chapters 28-2416 and 28-737 allow hybrid vehicle owners with an $8.00 special plates/hybrid sticker that is displayed on said vehicle to use the High Occupancy Vehicle (HOV) lanes regardless of the number of passengers. Arizona has not instituted this policy as it is awaiting clarification of the federal Hybrid HOV waiver from the Environmental Protection Agency.

**California**: Hybrid Car owners who have purchased their hybrids from San Jose dealers are exempt from local parking fees. For eligibility, contact Jason Burton (408) 794-1427, jason.burton@ci.sj.ca.us.

If you own a Zero Emission Vehicle or Super Ultra Low Emission Vehicle as defined by the California Air Resources Board, you may purchase a California Clean Air Vehicle Decal from the California Department of Motor Vehicles. Once you have purchased and affixed the decal to your vehicle per DMV instructions, you can park without depositing coins at on- and off-street metered parking spaces throughout the City of Los Angeles. For more information, visit:
http://www.lacity.org/LADOT/FreePark.htm

**Colorado**: The Colorado Department of Revenue offers a tax credit for the purchase of a hybrid electric vehicle (HEV), up to $4,713.00. For more information, including tax credit amounts for Model Year 2002 and 2003 HEVs, please visit www.revenue.state.co.us/fyi/html/income09.html. (Reference: Colorado Revised Statutes (CRS) §39-22-516 and §39-33-102.)

Colorado has passed legislation that would allow the hybrids to use the HOV lanes with single occupants. While a federal waiver has been passed, the Colorado Department of Transportation is analyzing that bill and state for compatibility. The EPA has up to 180 days to give the states guidelines for which vehicles would be allowed into HOV lanes pursuant to the new federal law.

**Connecticut**: The purchase of hybrid electric vehicles (HEVs) with a fuel economy rating of at least 40 miles per gallon (mpg) and the original purchase of dedicated natural gas, LPG, hydrogen, or electric vehicles are exempt from sales tax.

On June 6, 2005, the city of New Haven passed a law permitting hybrid vehicles registered in New Haven free parking at metered spots within the city. The ordinance will take effect within one month and only apply to alternative fuel vehicles registered in New Haven. Owners will have to come to City Hall to receive a decal which will be attached

---

[7] Appendix A is from http://www.hybridcars.com/tax-deductions-credits.html

to the vehicle. Motorists will still need to obey posted time limits and must park in legal spots. For more information contact DSlap@Newhavenct.net

**District of Columbia**: Within the DMV Reform Amendment Act Of 2004 went into effect on April 15, 2005. One provision exempts owners of hybrid and other alternative fuel vehicles from excise tax on their vehicle, and will reduce the vehicle registration charge, while excise tax rates for heavy passenger vehicles (over 5,000 pounds) will increase to 8% (from 7%). For more information, contact Elizabeth.Berry@dc.gov or Corey.Buffo@dc.gov

**Florida**: Inherently low-emission vehicles (ILEVs) and hybrid electric vehicles (HEVs) may be driven in high occupancy vehicle (HOV) lanes at any time regardless of vehicle occupancy. ILEVs and HEVs that are certified and labeled in accordance with federal regulations may be driven in HOV lanes at any time, regardless of the number of passengers in the vehicle. The vehicle must have a decal issued by the Florida Division of Motor Vehicles, obtained for a $5 fee, which must be renewed annually. For more information, please contact the Florida Division of Motor Vehicles at dmv@hsmv.state.fl.us or (850) 922-9000. (Reference Florida Statutes 316.0741)

**Georgia:** Hybrid electric vehicles (HEVs) shall be authorized to use high occupancy vehicle lanes, regardless of the number of passengers if the U.S. Congress or U.S. Department of Transportation approve such authorization through legislative or regulatory action. (Reference Georgia Code Section 32-9-4) The term 'alternative fuel vehicle' is expanded to include HEVs. A HEV is defined as a motor vehicle, which draws propulsion energy from onboard sources of stored energy, which include an internal combustion or heat engine using combustible fuel and a rechargeable energy storage system. HEVs must also meet federal Clean Air Act and California emissions standards and must have a fuel economy that is 1.5 times the Model Year 2002 EPA composite class average for the same vehicle class. (Reference Georgia Code Section 40-2-76)

**Illinois:** The Illinois Alternate Fuels Rebate Program (Rebate Program) provides rebates for 80% of the incremental cost of purchasing an AFV or converting a vehicle to operate on an alternative fuel. The maximum amount of each rebate is $4,000. Eligible vehicles include natural gas, propane, and electric. Gasoline-electric hybrid vehicles are not eligible.

**Louisiana**: The Louisiana Department of Natural Resources offers a state income tax credit worth 20% of the cost of converting a vehicle to operate on an alternative fuel, and 20% of the incremental cost of purchasing an Original Equipment Manufacturer (OEM) alternative fuel vehicle (AFV). For the purchase of an OEM AFV, the tax credit cannot exceed the lesser of 2% of the total cost of the vehicle or $1,500. Only those vehicles registered in Louisiana can receive the tax credit. For more information, please contact the Louisiana Department of Natural Resources at (225) 342-1399 or the Louisiana Department of Revenue at (225) 219-0102, option 2. (Reference Revised Statutes (RS) S47:38 and S47:287.757). The Louisiana department of revenue concluded that "The cost of equipment involved in converting to a hybrid vehicle or installed by a manufacturer of hybrid vehicles can be used to compute this credit." Note: The Revenue Ruling No. 02-019 November 8, 2002 established the department's position on allowing hybrids vehicles to receive this credit. However, a Revenue Ruling does not have the force and effect of law and is not binding on the public. It is a statement of the department's position and is binding on the department until superseded or modified by a subsequent change in statute, regulation, declaratory ruling, or court decision.

**Maine:** Maine law pursuant to MRSA 36, sections 1752 and 1760-79 allows a partial sales tax credit of approximately $500 for hybrid cars that do not have a comparable vehicle model, such as the Toyota Prius and Honda Insight. It allows a credit of approximately $300 for cars that have a comparable gasoline-powered model, such as the hybrid Honda Civic. For more information, contact Lynne Cayting of the Department of Environmental Protection at (207) 287-7599, or via email at lynne.a.cayting@state.me.us For information about the tax exemption for hybrid electric vehicles, visit www.maineenvironment.org/energy/TaxCredit.htm. Download form at http://www.state.me.us/revenue/forms/sales/str46a.pdf

**Maryland:** Maryland H.B. 61 exempts qualified hybrid electric vehicles from motor vehicle emissions testing requirements.

Owners of hybrid cars will get discounts on parking at the 15 city-owned parking garages in Baltimore. The plan cuts between 32- and 85 dollars from the monthly fees for owners of the fuel-efficient vehicles. Baltimore will limit participation to 200 vehicles and the program will apply only to monthly, contract parking. Drivers of the three most fuel-efficient models can apply for a decal that will let them park in designated spots in the city's garages.

**Massachusetts:** For the years 2006-2010, individuals that purchase a hybrid or alternative fuel vehicle, which can be powered by ethanol, low-sulfur diesel, compressed natural gas, liquefied natural gas, and hydrogen will register for a special placard and receive a number of incentives, including: an income tax deduction of $2000; the right to travel in HOV lanes regardless of passengers; and discounts or free parking in municipalities which choose to participate.

The bill will require that five percent of all new state agency "fleet vehicles" be hybrids or run on alternative fuel, with 50 percent of the state fleet reliant on alternative fuels by 2010. A $10 million bond would establish a fund controlled by the Division of Energy Resources to assist municipalities and regional transit authorities in building alternative fuel stations on public lands and acquiring alternative fuel vehicles or hybrids.

Corporations with fleets of more than 50 comprised of at least 10 percent alternative fuel vehicles would receive a tax credit of half the difference in price between those vehicles and their conventional gasoline counterparts.

**New Jersey**: On May 4, 2006, the New Jersey Turnpike Authority, which administers the turnpike and the Garden State Parkway, voted to allow hybrid vehicles to use the high occupancy vehicles lanes on the turnpike. The ruling's effect may be limited since the turnpike, which sees an average of 700,000 drivers daily, has HOV lanes only between Interchange 11 in Woodbridge and Interchange 14 in Newark going both northbound and southbound. The Garden State Parkway does not have car pool lanes.

Decals are not required. Turnpike Authority officials said state police do not anticipate any problems identifying which cars are hybrids

**New Mexico**: Hybrid electric vehicles (HEVs) with a U.S. Environmental Protection Agency (EPA) fuel economy rating of at least 27.5 miles per gallon are eligible for a one-time exemption from the motor vehicle excise tax and state sales tax.

In Albuquerque, hybrid cars are exempt from parking meter fees. For more information, visit: http://www.cabq.gov/parking/HybridPermits.html.
Or call The City of Albuquerque's parking office at 505-924-3950. Contact Deborah James: Djames@cabq.gov (505) 768-3036

**New York**: New York's Alternative Fuel (Clean Fuel) Vehicle Tax Incentive Program, which offered tax credits and a tax exemption for purchasing new hybrid electric vehicles (HEVs), have expired. In Jan. 2006, Governor Pataki proposed new incentives. For more information, please contact the New York State Energy Research & Development Authority (NYSERDA) at 866- NYSERDA, via email at info@nyserda.org or visit the web site at www.nyserda.org

Clean Pass is a program allowing eligible low-emission, energy-efficient vehicles to use the 40-mile Long Island Expressway High Occupancy Vehicle (LIE/HOV). Clean Pass is a multi-agency pilot program partnering three New York State agencies, the State Department of Transportation (NYSDOT), the State Department of Motor Vehicles (DMV), and State Department of Environmental Conservation (DEC).

**Oregon**: A Residential Tax Credit of up to $1,500 is available for the purchase of a HEV or dual-fuel vehicle. For more information, contact Deby Davis of the Oregon Department of Energy at (503) 378-8351, via email at deby.s.davis@state.or.us You can also find detailed information about qualifying vehicles at: http://egov.oregon.gov/ENERGY/TRANS/hybridcr.shtml

A Business Energy Tax Credit is available for the purchase of hybrid electric vehicles (HEVs) and dual-fuel vehicles, the cost of converting vehicles to operate on an alternative fuel, and the cost of constructing alternative fuel refueling stations. The tax credit is 35% of the incremental cost of the system or equipment and is taken over five years. For more information, please contact Justin Klure of the Oregon Department of

Energy at (503) 373-1581, via email at justin.klure@state.or.us or visit the Web site at www.energy.state.or.us

**Pennsylvania**: Pennsylvania's Department of Environmental Protection will offer an opportunity to Commonwealth residents to apply for a rebate to assist with the incremental cost for the purchase of a new hybrid, bi-fuel, dual-fuel or dedicated alternative fuel vehicle. The rebate amount is $500. The rebate will be offered as long as funds are available. Rebates will be offered on a "first come, first served" basis. Rebate applications shall be submitted no later than six months after the purchase.

Press release issued by the Commonwealth of Pennsylvania on March 9, 2006: The program has been so successful; the state is expected to run out of rebate money sometime in April. DEP Secretary Kathleen A. McGinty said the commonwealth already has awarded more than $1.3 million in rebates from the $1.5 million allotted for the program for the 2005-06 fiscal years. Another $1 million will become available for the fiscal year beginning July 1. Because buyers have six months from the time of the purchase to apply for the rebates, people buying hybrid electric and alternative fuel vehicles after the current funding runs out still will be able to apply for rebates when the programs reopens. For more information, visit www.dep.state.pa.us

**Texas:** The City of Austin's "Drive Clean--Park Free" program gives city-registered owners of hybrid vehicles that receive an EPA air pollution score of 8 or better a $100 pre-paid parking cards to park in any of the city's 3,700 parking meters. Owners must submit an application to the city and receive a bumper sticker showing their participation in the program. Eligible vehicles must be purchased at certified dealerships within the Austin City Limits. For more information go to http://www.ci.austin.tx.us/airquality/parkfree.htm

**Utah**: The state provides an income tax credit for 50% of the incremental cost ($3,000 maximum) of a clean-fuel vehicle built by an OEM and/or an income tax credit for 50% of the cost ($2,500 maximum) of the after-market conversion of vehicles purchased after January 1, 2001 and registered in Utah. If not previously used, the tax credit on used vehicles may be claimed. Tax credits are available for businesses and individuals and may be carried forward up to five years. Tax credits are not available for electric hybrids, except the Honda Civic hybrid. Documentation must be provided as described in the Utah state tax form TC-40V. For more information, please contact Ran Macdonald of the Utah Division of Air Quality at (801) 536-4071, or via email at rmacdonald@utah.gov (Reference Utah Code 59-7-605 and 59-10-127).

Vehicles with clean fuel group license plates are authorized to travel in HOV lanes regardless of the number of occupants. The clean fuel plate may be purchased for $10 from any Motor Vehicle Division office by presenting a clean special fuel certificate. This incentive expires December 31, 2005. For more information, please contact the Utah State Tax Commission's Motor Vehicle Division at (800) DMV-UTAH or (801) 297-

7780, or visit the Web site at www.dmv.utah.gov/licensespecialplates.html (Reference Utah Code 41-1a-1211, 41-6-53.5, and 63-55-241).

On Aug. 11, Mayor Rocky Anderson scheduled a meeting with top city officials to discuss the creation of a free parking incentive for hybrid vehicles in Salt Lake City. City transportation engineer Kevin Young confirmed to the Desert Morning News that his department has prepared an ordinance that would enact the free parking.

**Virginia:** AFVs displaying the Virginia 'Clean Special Fuels' license plate can use the Virginia HOV lanes, regardless of the number of occupants, until July 1, 2006. Dedicated AFVs and the Toyota Prius, and Honda Insight and Civic hybrid electric vehicles qualify. For more information, please visit the Virginia Department of Motor Vehicles Web site at www.dmv.state.va.us/webdoc/citizen/vehicles/cleanspecialfuel.asp (Reference Virginia Code §33.1-46.2 and §46.2-749.3)

**Washington:** Electric, CNG, and LPG vehicles are exempt from emission control inspections. Effective June 13, 2002, hybrid motor vehicles that obtain a rating by the U.S. Environmental Protection Agency of at least 50 miles per gallon of gas during city driving are also exempt from these inspections. (Reference RCW 46.16.015)

**West Virginia:** The State of West Virginia allows a credit for the purchase of a new motor vehicle that runs on an alternative fuel or for the conversion of a traditionally fueled motor vehicle to an alternatively fueled motor vehicle. Alternative fuel types include compressed natural gas, liquefied natural gas, liquefied petroleum, methanol, ethanol, coal-derived liquid fuels, electricity, solar energy and fuel mixtures containing at least 85 percent alcohol. The tax department includes hybrids in this tax credit. Print out the necessary tax form. For more information see: http://www.state.wv.us/taxdiv

Mr. ISSA. We are privileged to have here today Dr. Andrew Frank, director, University of California at Davis, Hybrid Electric Research Center; Mr. David Hermance, executive engineer, Toyota Motor North America—and, yes, mine happen to all be Toyota. But I am looking forward to hearing more from Mr. John German, manager, Environmental and Energy Analyses, American Honda Motor Co.; and Mr. Don MacKenzie, vehicles engineer, Union of Concerned Scientists.

I am looking forward to your testimonies; and particularly, since we have those in the record, I ask unanimous consent that the briefing memo prepared by the subcommittee staff be inserted into the record as well as all relevant materials.

I additionally ask that your written statements all be placed in the record so that you need not do your opening statements verbatim but in fact can embellish or short cut or add to, essentially get more than we got in writing.

I now would turn to the ranking member, but instead what we will do is I will ask that the panel be sworn in. As soon as the ranking member arrives, she may choose to insert her opening statement into the record or at that time may give her opening statement.

I would ask you at this time to please rise to take your oath and raise your right hands. I mention this is a rule that we do to everybody, not just auto companies. We do it to university professors, too, I guess is what I'm trying to say.

[Witnesses sworn.]

Mr. ISSA. The record will show all answered in the affirmative. Please be seated.

Dr. Frank, we have introduced you. We haven't begun to say enough about how pleased we are to have you here. Before this began, you did one-up me, by letting me know that you had already created a hybrid vehicle in 1971 before I first saw the technology coming out of the University of Michigan in 1972. So, with that, I would like to learn more.

Please—normally, we say 5 minutes, but it is a plus or minus 5 minutes. There will be a light that will come on, and with 1 minute remaining it will go to yellow, and when it goes to red do not open any new thoughts.

Mr. FRANK. Hit me on the head with a hammer.

Mr. ISSA. No, no. We are the kinder, gentler Government Reform. We didn't even hit Sammy Sosa on the head.

## STATEMENTS OF ANDREW FRANK, DIRECTOR, UNIVERSITY OF CALIFORNIA-DAVIS, HYBRID ELECTRIC RESEARCH CENTER; DAVID HERMANCE, EXECUTIVE ENGINEER, TOYOTA MOTOR NORTH AMERICA; JOHN GERMAN, MANAGER, ENVIRON-MENTAL AND ENERGY ANALYSES, AMERICAN HONDA MOTOR CO.; AND DON MACKENZIE, VEHICLES ENGINEER, UNION OF CONCERNED SCIENTISTS

### STATEMENT OF ANDREW FRANK

Mr. FRANK. I am going to talk about hybrids and plug-in hybrids. I want to distinguish the difference between what the two are, and mostly I want to focus on environmental benefits, cost-effectiveness, market benefits, transition incentives, and U.S. manufacturing capacity.

The car companies and most research of hybrids of today use a relatively small battery pack. It has fuel economy up to 50 percent better, but it has no electric energy or not enough electric energy to drive the car all electrically for any substantial distance. The engine is downsized 10 or 20 percent.

But if you add a plug, then the question is, what is a plug-in hybrid? The plug-in hybrid is like a Toyota Prius, but it has a much smaller engine, much smaller—I am talking about half or less—and a much larger electric motor and larger batteries. But these batteries can be plugged in at 120 volt standard plugs. The most important thing is the combination allows the vehicle to actually have better performance and, of course, much better fuel economy.

But, really, we shouldn't be talking about fuel economy. We should be talking about fuel consumption. Because when you plug it in you are using energy from the wall rather than using gasoline, and that is the best way to get ourselves off the oil diet, as President Bush says.

So we call this all-electric range. All-electric range [AER], operates on batteries from 100 percent state of charge down to about 20 percent states of charge. Then when you stop driving you plug it in and the batteries fill up.

This is what a long-range, all-electric range or plug-in hybrid is all about. There is a much larger battery but much smaller gasoline engine. There is the conventional hybrid, and there is the 60-mile-range HEV. Sixty means that it is possible to build a car with 60 miles of all-electric range. This requires a lot of batteries, but the overall vehicle does not have to weigh any more.

We have already built these cars. They don't weigh any more because the engine is much smaller. But the most important thing is we add a plug. So the advantages of a large battery pack is it provides the ability for zero emission driving, and it does not have to be charged since the gasoline or diesel engine is always there. If you don't charge it, you just use more gasoline, but if you do charge it, you use one-tenth to one-third the cost of fuel. In other words, using electricity is like buying gasoline at 70 cents a gallon instead of $3 and going up. People will be plugging these cars in.

Mr. ISSA. Even in California?

Mr. FRANK. Even in California. In fact, all the numbers I will talk about are California numbers.

Batteries can be used to store energy from small wind, solar and water systems. In other words, you can have personal solar panels on your house, and today's sun will give you tomorrow's driving. And what that does is give individuals energy independence.

So here are some examples of solar panels that are built by the Ovonic Solar Co. specifically to charge automobiles.

The same thing will hold for wind. The problem with most renewable energy like wind and solar, however, is storage, but the plug-in hybrid gives you that storage, and it does not cost the utilities anything because the private person is paying for that.

Therefore, the plug-in hybrid provides the most efficient use of renewable energy; because in a conventional renewable energy, big solar and wind, when the sun shines or the wind blows, you have to shut down a power plant somewhere because every electron you generate has to be used; and when you shut down a power plant, that makes the power plant less efficient.

In this case, with a plug-in hybrid, you have a place to put that energy, and that is in the car. So a plug-in hybrid makes the renewable energy much more cost effective.

Additional use batteries can be charged at night, thus balancing the electric grid, making the electric grid actually more efficient. The electric charging does not have to be done with anything special. A standard plug, 120 volts with GFI, is all you need. So we can reduce gasoline consumption by 80–90 percent just by charging the cars with a standard 120 volt plug. That is not using any solar.

So here are some results of a study that was done by EPRI, the Electric Power Research Institute, but I must say this is not solar electric power. The DOE, General Motors and other California agencies were involved in this study, and the results are a compilation of U.S. DOE labs and car companies and, of course, the universities. That's me.

On the left hand side is the fuel costs—the CV means conventional vehicle; and the HEV zero is a conventional hybrid like a Prius.

The upshot of all these curves is the more batteries you have, the more benefits. More batteries means that $CO_2$ and smog decreases.

This is a market preference, and the objective is to get to 50 percent.

I am going to skip ahead.

And this is the most important one. This is the annual fuel consumption [referring to power point presentation]. The annual fuel consumption goes down. This is for SUVs all the way down to compact cars.

Notice once you get out to 60 miles all-electric range that the amount of fuel used is one-quarter of a compact Ford Focus. This is the amount of gasoline saved.

If we could get 10 percent of the fleet of HEV 40's—by the way, that is the number chosen by President Bush—we would reduce oil consumption by about 300 million barrels a year. That is about 4.5 percent of the U.S. oil used per year, and we would be out of the Middle East.

So that is the diesel, [again referring to power point] and I am going to skip right to the conclusions.

We can reduce the Mideast imports. Plug-in hybrids can use solar and other renewables, and plug-in hybrids allow us to integrate—here is an important feature—integrate both transportation and stationary energy use for an overall society that is much more efficient. We need to convince the car companies to make these things, and maybe they are convinced already. We need to create public demand for these, and we need to construct at least 1,500 more demonstration vehicles.

I'm sorry to overrun.

[The prepared statement of Mr. Frank follows:]

**Testimony for Congress**
**The House of Representatives Committee on Gov. Reform**
**Subcommittee on Energy and Resources**
**on the**
**Environmental Benefits, Cost Effectiveness, Market Penetration/Incentives,**
**and US Manufacturing Capacity**
**of**
**Hybrid Electric and Plug-In Hybrid Electric Vehicles**

**By**

**Professor Andrew A. Frank**
**University of California-Davis**
**Dept. of Mech. Aero. Eng.**
**One Shields Ave, Davis, CA 95616**
**Tel:530 752 8120, fax: 530 752 4158**

This report is written for the House of Representatives, Congress of the United States, Committee on Government Reform, Subcommittee on Energy and Resources for testimony to be given on July 20, 2006 at 2 pm.

This report will assume the Congress is already informed on the concept of the Hybrid Electric Vehicle (HEV) and the more advanced Plug-In Hybrid Electric Vehicle (PHEV).

I will briefly describe the difference between the HEV and the PHEV. The PHEV is not simply a HEV with more batteries. It can only be successful if the larger battery capacity is integrated with a bigger electric motor and a smaller gasoline engine. The results, shown in the figures below indicate fuel economy improvement of 50% over a conventional hybrid and 100% over a conventional car when using gasoline only after it has depleted it's battery to the maintenance state of charge (SOC) of around 20%. This is also dependent on the size of the battery pack.

In addition the PHEV needs only a 120 volt 15 amp standard GFI plug and circuit to charge. Thus the charger can become very low cost and use commonly available standard electrical outlets. This can be implemented for the smallest vehicle to the largest SUV. The PHEV is dependent on the driver to plug in the vehicle to reap the full benefits of displaced fuel. The driver of these cars will find a plug whenever they are parked because the cost of electricity to run these cars is about ¼ the cost of buying gasoline at $3.00/gallon for gasoline. They already use ½ the gasoline per mile after the batteries are depleted. Thus, the proper metric to judge the PHEV is the total gasoline fuel used for annual driving and the total electricity used annually. This metric has not yet been set by the USDOE and USEPA. This and other regulatory items will have to evaluated by EPA and other regulatory sources for the PHEV since it uses two energy sources.

A two year study published in 2001 by the Electric Power Research Institute (EPRI) under the guidance of a joint task force consisting of University, Federal Government Laboratories, Auto Industry, State Agencies, and Electric Utilities, Titled: "Comparing Hybrid Vehicle Options" will be referenced for the data presented in this report.

I have been researching Hybrid Electric Vehicles for the last 30 years and have constructed over a dozen such vehicles to prove the principal of increased fuel economy and performance and decreased emissions and green house gasses. These vehicles were constructed to show that the technology is feasible and cost effective if properly implemented. We have demonstrated in the vehicles that there is at least one way to build PHEV's that get double the fuel economy of the conventional car but yet provides greater performance and much lower operating costs.

As a result of my experience with the USDOE National Labs Argonne, and NREL, DARPA, and many of the car companies both domestic and abroad, I have developed the knowledge of the technology choices that are currently available and the technologies necessary to manufacture the components and produce the vehicles for mass consumption. In particular, the HEV and PHEV concepts in this report are all to be built on conventional vehicle platforms from compact to full size sedans, (Example, Ford Focus to the Ford 500), and small SUV's and vans to full size Pickup trucks and SUV's, (Example, Ford Escape to the Ford Expedition).

The emissions and gasoline reduction of these vehicles are summarized in the collection of Figures below.

(The HEV20 and HEV60 are PHEV's with 20 and 60 miles of electric drive capability on the Federal Urban Driving Cycle, FUDC. This is the driving cycle used by the US EPA for emissions and fuel economy rating of all light duty vehicles, the CV means Conventional Vehicles and the HEV0 is equivalent to a Toyota Prius.)

The first figure shows 4 graphs depicting the Fuel costs based on $1.50/gallon Gasoline at the time of the study and the cost of electricity @ 6cents/kwhr from the California Electric Utility Grid, the $CO_2$ green house gases, the equivalent miles per gallon and the smog precursors.
These graphs constructed by simulation for a 3300 lb family sedan the size of a Chevrolet Lumina or Ford Taurus.

# ar Co's.-DOE Labs study "Compari )ptions"– for a 1500kg car

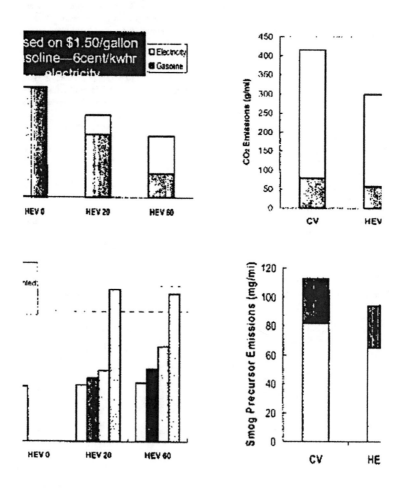

iclature for these graphs are as follows:

# I, Running, Component and Purcha
# for Midsize 1500 kg car, in 2001,@

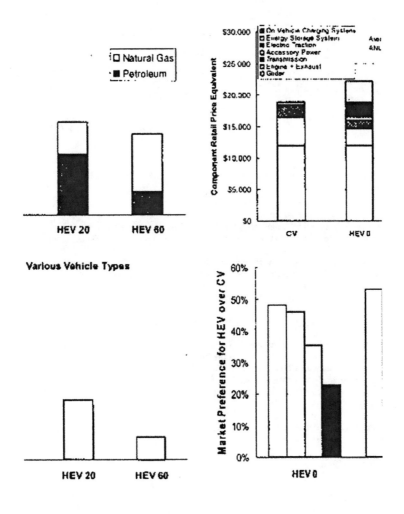

graphs:

Mid-size HEV car Market Potential vs. Price

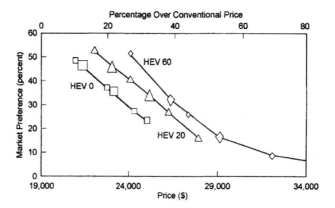

Legend:
Horizontal scale is retail price for the vehicles. The base 2001 vehicle is $19,000.
Vertical scale shows percent of new car sales based on a survey of 400 people. The
curves show the price-volume relationship of the vehicles and will help determine the
subsidy needed obtain a new car penetration percentage for a mid size family sedan.

This set of curves indicate how the pricing of these vehicles will affect the sales volume
compared to the conventional car of identical size and performance. For example to
achieve a 50% penetration the retail price of a 60 mile range PHEV must be priced at
about $5000 over the conventional vehicle. The reason for this is because the people in
the survey are willing to pay d=for the additional features of the PHEV such as going to
the gas station only 4 times a year versus 35 times a year in a conventional car.

Other features that have been developed since this study will give the PHEV even more
value. For example, the integration of the PHEV with solar panels and small wind
turbines on the roofs of the home and office will give the user energy independence over
the electric grid and the gas station. This feature and other newly developed uses for the
PHEV has not been included thus the results shown are conservative, and people will
likely pay more for the PHEV.

The next curve show the green house gas emissions for all classes of light duty passenger
vehicles, pickup trucks and SUV's.

# s Emissions for all light duty cars

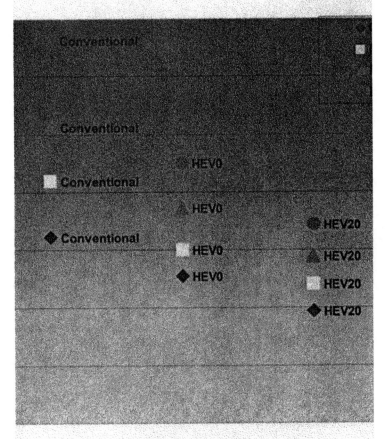

**Increasing Hybridization →**

EV cars are currently evaluated. This means
ed to be developed to judge the merits of the

## e Consumption for 12,000 miles of vehicles

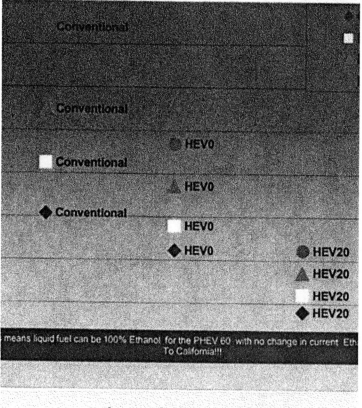

**Increasing Hybridization →**

asoline saved for the average c
V, PHEV's as a function of AEI
ested standard for AER specifi
entional car uses 740 gals gasc

**asoline Saved for Different All-Electric Rang**

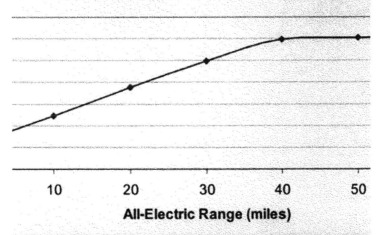

**All-Electric Range (miles)**

ings for 10% fleet penetration (PHEV-
els saving 4.5% of the US oil used/yea
liminate Middle Eastern Oil Imports !!
anol in PHEV's further increases oil s
ept is to construct PHEV's with flex fu

It should be noted that as the batteries are increased for longer AER in the PHEV, the electric motor power is also increased and the gasoline engine is decreased proportionally for the same performance. Surprisingly the weight is nearly the same as the batteries are increased for AER since the gasoline engine becomes smaller and lighter and the vehicle powertrain becomes simpler and less complex.

### Market Penetration and Incentives:

It should be noted that the incremental cost of the PHEV over a conventional gasoline automatic car at 100,000 units is a function of the AER since the incremental costs is dominated by the costs of batteries. The maximum range considered to be practical and within the range of acceptable consumer reach is 60 miles. This is reasonable since the average vehicle in the US travels 40 miles per day and about 15,000 miles a year.

The AER of a HEV or PHEV can be a minimum of 10 miles to 60 miles. This range of AER is considered to be practical for the average vehicle user. This range will save gasoline depending on AER. The graphs show that the longer the AER the greater the gasoline displacement with electricity. It is assumed that driver of these vehicles will plug them in to use electricity because they can travel 4 times farther for the same dollar cost. Or using electricity to power the car is 1/4 the cost of gasoline at $3/gallon. Thus, the driver has an economic incentive to plug this car in and use electric energy to displace as much gasoline as he can. This incentive rises as the cost of gasoline goes up.

With this simple cost driver for the PHEV, the subsidy required of the government is relatively small if the cost projections are close. The manufacturers however, will have to make a tooling investment and pay for development costs which must be recovered in a relatively short period of time. Thus the initial cost must be higher than estimated because the volume of 100,000 PHEV's per year will not be achieved for at least 5 years for each manufacturer. This means there will have to be some dollar cost subsidy for at least this period of time as the volume of HEV and PHEV's are increased.

To meet cost parity with a conventional car or truck in the beginning, it may require as much as 30% of the base vehicle costs for a 60 mile AER PHEV until the volume gets to over 100,000 vehicles per year. At 100,000 vehicles per year the incremental cost could come down to as little as 10% for the PHEV 60. This is due to anticipated lower cost and durability of the batteries and the continued rise of gasoline cost and anticipated possible gasoline disruptions.

An added incentive for the purchase of the PHEV is that such a car or truck can be powered for daily travel by **personal** Solar and Wind generators at about 30% of the vehicle cost up front. This would give the individual users **energy independence** for the life of the solar or wind generator of about 30 years. The cost of fuel using personal solar or wind for the average car will drop from about 15 cents per mile for $3.00/gallon gasoline to 2 cents per mile for a solar array on top of his house or office. An incentive from the Government to buy solar or wind generators for powering the PHEV can bring this combination technology to the market quickly. This concept also allows the excess energy generated to supplement the electric load of their home or office. In addition to **personal energy independence**, the US will benefit from greatly reduced petroleum and coal use.

## US manufacturing capability to produce HEVand PHEV

The vehicle manufacturing capability of the US is currently greatly underutilized due to a shift in vehicle preference for more fuel efficient and reliable vehicles. The American car manufacturing companies have focused on large vehicles with the expectation that oil prices will remain stable at less than $50/ barrel. This strategy has led to low sales and plant closures.

Even when they have introduced hybrids they have chosen the wrong market, focusing on the larger vehicles and have chosen the most expensive technology. The example is the Ford Escape hybrid using Toyota/Aisin A/W technology, where the fuel economy is 35 mpg but the Toyota Prius gets 50 mpg. The Ford Escape hybrid is technically the same as the Prius but it is over 1000 lbs heavier. And it is better than the standard Escape in fuel economy by 50%.

However, the general public does not see these details as a limitation and thus misjudge the Escape as inferior technology to the Toyota and therefore the sales volume is falling short of expectations. The lesson learned here should be that the American public is comparing only raw fuel economy numbers independent of vehicle size and features. Costs of the complex hybrid systems is also high.

Thus the American manufacturing problem is in both lower cost technology and in choosing the right platform for the competition with Japan. There seems to be a movement toward selecting a better platform for a Plug-In hybrid at General Motors in a recent announcement of a 55 mpg PHEV to be in production by 2008 model year. The cost may not be competitive with Toyota since Toyota has already gone through three generations and are busy on a more advance PHEV with lower cost componenrts although no production date or configuration has been announced.

The only way the American car companies can compete on the same class vehicle is to introduce a lower cost, simpler but more sophisticated powertrain system. They all have selected a two motor-CVT system which is more expensive than the Toyota system. While they may be researching simpler one motor-CVT systems, there is no indication that such a system is being considered. In addition, the mechanical CVT for the HEV and PHEV has largely been ignored by the American Car companies because of some bad experiences with mechanical CVT's in the past. The bad experiences came from a lack of understanding of the CVT technology and the unwillingness of the American OEM's to fully adopt technology developed outside their laboratories. When this was tried the OEM's requirements were beyond what the technology could handle but the OEM's were unwilling to invest their own resources to understand the real problems and go through the development process themselves. Thus at least three plant investments have been made at Billons of dollars and abandoned. Yet, there are numerous European and Japanese vehicles with CVT's but only the American Ford 500 is currently in production with a CVT under license and Joint Venture from ZF Transmission of Germany. Ford has not developed its' own system. Advance CVT technology and concepts are available in the USA and developed under a electric drive project for DARPA about 5 years ago, but no manufacturer has currently adopted the technology for production development.

It is the opinion of the Author that the Mechanical CVT is the critical technology needed for a low cost HEV and PHEV. Some of this technology has already been licensed to Japanese firms who have invested the research to prove and develop durability, low noise and much higher efficiency. There is much more Intellectual Property in this area available in this country that could be adopted by the American OEM's.

## Conclusion

We have discussed the following issues and provided the data which shows the benefits of the HEV and PHEV technology.
1. The effectiveness of the HEV and PHEV for fuel, and emissions reduction.
2. The market—price relationship of the HEV and PHEV20 and PHEV60 relative to the conventional car or CV. Obviously, the technology must be priced to sell to the customers and to do any good for the US situation of imported oil it must be done in volume. Thus a target of 50% market penetration should be the goal. The author feels that initially a subsidy from the government is needed for industry to have the incentive to make the investment in this country. Foreign companies with long range planning and goals have already begun, thus the US will have to move quickly to catch up. The PHEV gives the American companies a chance to leap ahead of Japan in technology, but they must move quickly or they will be buying from Toyota again and lose more market share.
3. The use of the PHEV advanced system to move immediately toward oil independence by combining vehicle electric energy use with direct small privately owned renewable energy systems such as Solar and Wind becomes possible with the PHEV. This adds value to the concept and people have not yet fully become aware of this possibility.
4. The manufacturing capability of the American auto companies and industry is available to adopt the PHEV technology TODAY but the will to make the investment in R&D is not there even though their market share continues to erode. Thus public government support is needed.
5. Further education of the public is needed to create the demand for the PHEV. Features such as a stable ¼ cost of energy using electricity for transportation instead of the fluctuating cost of gasoline, and the possibility of personal energy independence needs to be in the forefront of the American public to create the demand.
6. The penetration of the PHEV concept into our transportation fleet and the effect on oil imports is presented. It must be remembered that we currently replace less

11

than 10 percent of our fleet of vehicles a year and unless earlier retirement of vehicles is encouraged, we can at best begin fleet replacement about 2% a year. Meaning a minimum of 5 years to get 10% penetration.

7. We would have the most impact on oil reduction if the vehicles sold to the public were PHEV40 to PHEV60 type. The current industry thoughts are PHEV10 to PHEV20.

8. Congress needs to set incentives to encourage the PHEV40 to PHEV 60 for initial introduction for the fastest response to the issues of imported oil, Global Warming, and energy independence/security.

Energy independence with the PHEV40 or the PHEV60 can be achieve by one individual at a time but lead to a much more affluent society because the cost of energy can be reduced to virtually zero with an enhanced and advanced life style for the American People.

I will be happy to entertain further questions on the issues of producing the PHEV for the introduction to the American Market.

America needs to take the lead to show the world we can reduce our oil consumption and respond to the Global Warming threat with immediate action.

I will be happy to answer further questions about the technology and how best to move our car companies toward the PHEV and begin the reduction of our oil addiction.

v A. Frank

tric Vehicle Center

. Aero. Eng

Calif.-Davis

'52 8120

ot within a

ge range

robust

ny up to

**1.5X, Uses**

energy.

nsized 10%

ual

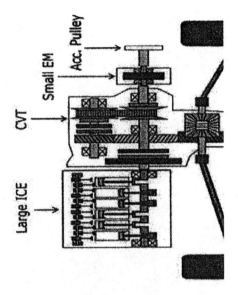

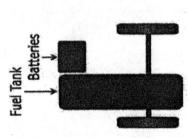

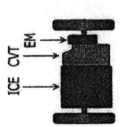

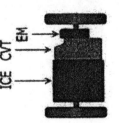

# What is a Plug-In HEV??

- The Plug-In HEV is like a Toyota Prius except it has a **smaller** engine and a **larger** electric motor and battery pack and **a plug** to the wall to charge the batteries with conventional 120v plugs!!

- This combination allows the vehicle to have **better** fuel economy, **higher** performance, and **All Electric Range** (AER) up to 60 miles with a **much simpler** powertrain and **no increase in weight**.

- AER is done with batteries from 100% SOC to 20% SOC then the engine maintains at 20% SOC. Then when you stop driving you plug-in and fill the batteries from the wall. If you don't plug-in you simply use more liquid fuel. No loss in performance!!

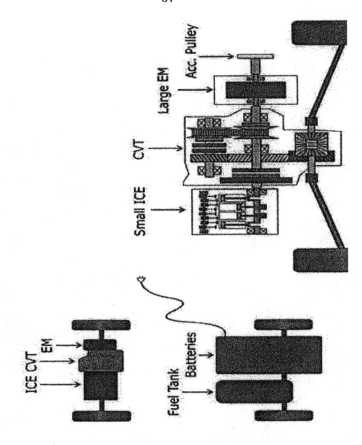

energy
to 90%
parts.
to CV
0% wall
-10%
ually.
mance
onal
ible

# The advantages of a large battery pack

- Provides ability to travel at Zero Emissions and low Noise for a substantial part or all of the vehicle's daily use.

- Does not have to be charged since the gasoline or diesel engine is always there to automatically take over when the charge gets below a set State of Charge (SOC), like 20%.

- **1/10th to 1/3 Fuel cost** for a PHEV running on Electricity obtained from the wall plug. $0.25-$1/eq gal

- **People will plug these cars in!!**

- **Batteries can be used to *store energy* from small wind, solar and water systems as well thus also making these systems More practical now! And even lower cost/mile!! Conv cars 14c/mi---PHEV 2c/mi !!!**

10 kW EV Charging Station

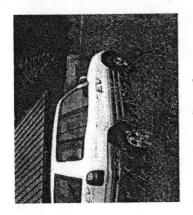

harging Station

# Problem with most Renewable energy generators—Storage!!

- Must have some form of energy storage because the renewables such as wind and solar are not consistent.

- To feed the grid, requires massive storage capability—A large cost!!

- The PHEV provides most efficient use of Renewable energy sources

- The PHEV makes Renewable Energy much **more cost effective** because they displace ever more expensive oil and coal.

## Additional uses for the large battery systems

- Batteries can be charged at night thus **balancing the electric grid** and raising the base load and reducing peak load generation with rolling reserves, thus reducing the cost of electricity to everyone!!

- Electric charging of the PHEV can be done at a **low power level, 1.5 to 2kw** , so there is no need for special charging stations. Standard 120 V GFI outlets will do. The standard Block heater plugs in some towns will do just fine!

Gasoline reduction on an annual basis can be up to 80% to 90% . **Therefore;** The liquid fuel for these vehicles can easily be Ethanol/Bio-Diesel. Thus Reducing Petroleum Consumption to ZERO NOW!! Without having to go to H2!!

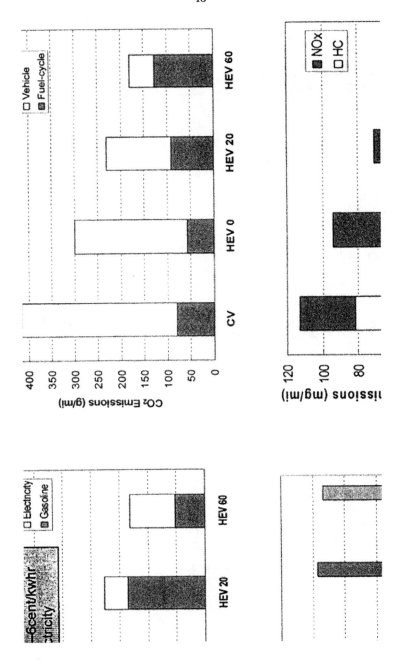

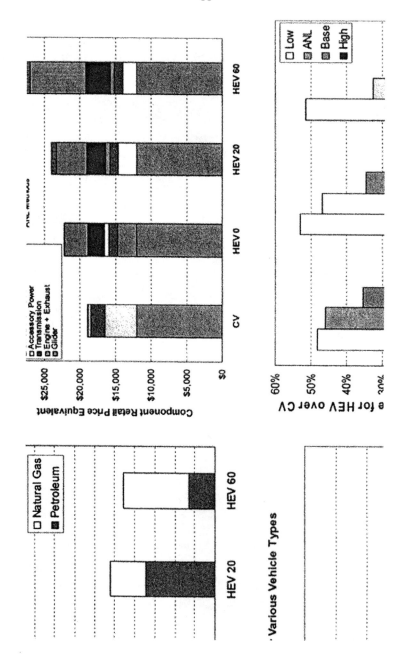

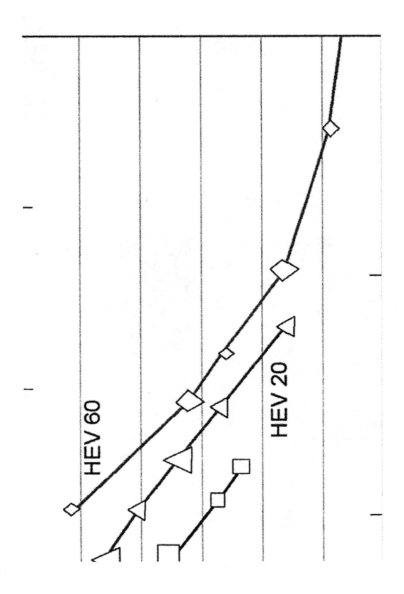

'94 Mercury Sable
60 mi AER, 58 mpg
Automatic mechanical
CVT

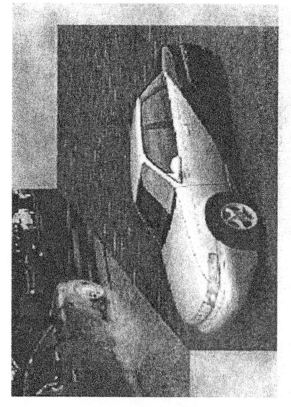

48

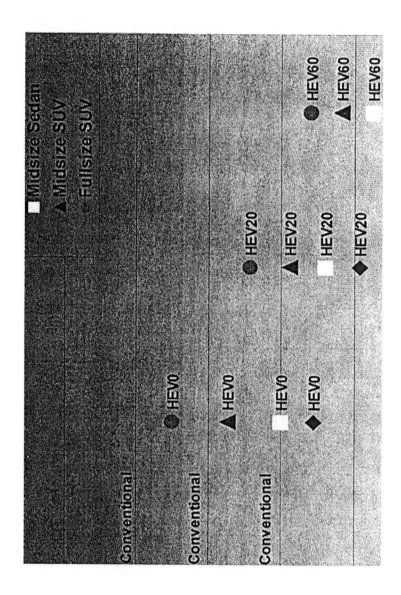

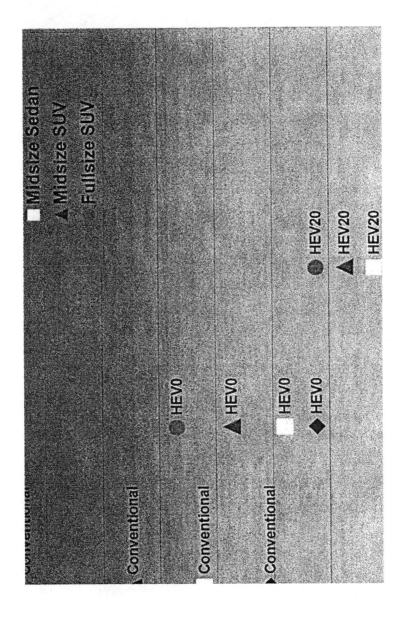

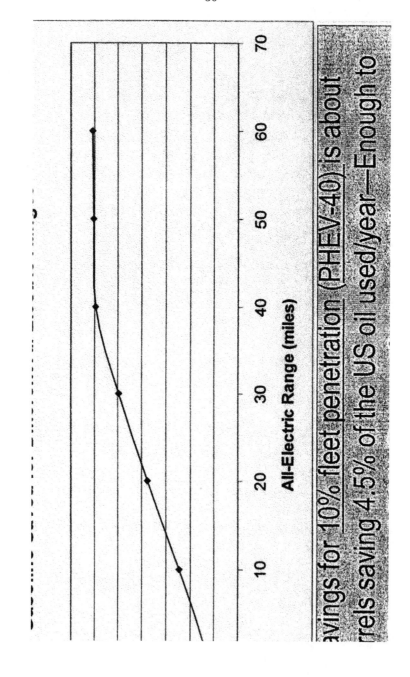

All-Electric Range (miles)

...avings for 10% fleet penetration (PHEV-40) is about ...rrels saving 4.5% of the US oil used/year—Enough to

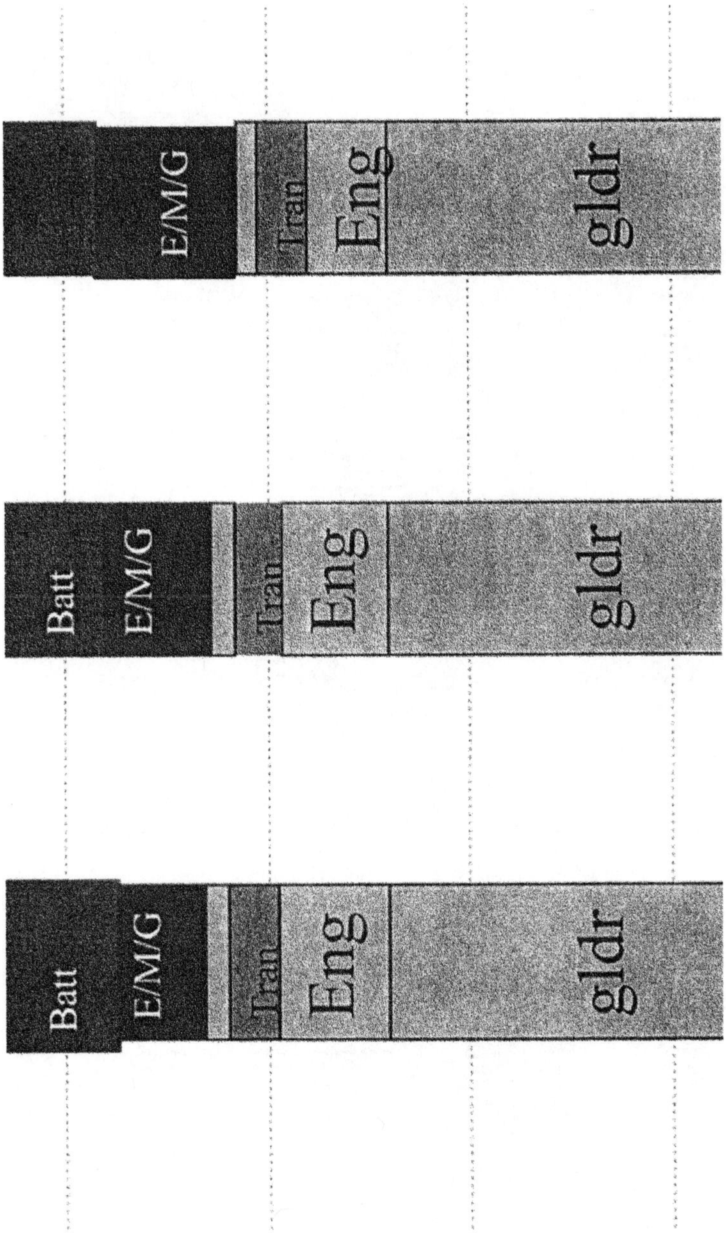
E/M/G
Tran
Eng
gldr
Batt
E/M/G
Tran
Eng
gldr
Batt
E/M/G
Tran
Eng
gldr

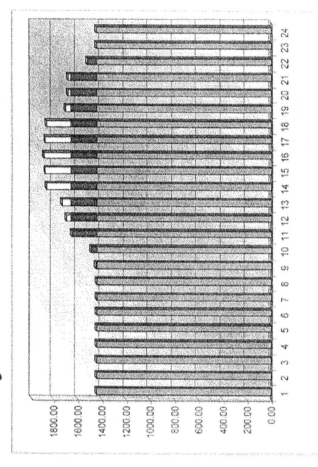

r plants!! --20 years at least!!

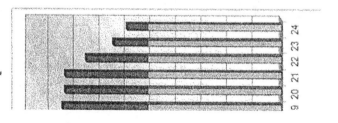

## Oil & Coal Reduction by using the PHEV as the Technology Center Piece

- Use, **home** wind, water and solar to charge batteries thus making new businesses. Driving fuel costs $\rightarrow$ 0

- Use PHEV batteries for **Home & Office** energy.

- Use PHEV batteries to balance electric grid to reduce electric power transmission costs.

- Burn ethanol from celluloustic biomaterials or bio-Diesel instead of petroleum derived fuel since PHEV uses 1/5th to 1/10th the fuel of a Conv. Vehicle.

Use PHEV for all energy supplied by renewable sources To Eventually Reduce per capita petroleum energy to near Zero while providing an even More advanced lifestyle.

# Summary and Conclusions

- PHEV's are a low cost solution to environmental & Energy Security problems and could provide high profits and employment for early investors.

- These vehicles can be brought to production now with little investment in development. No change in manufacturing and fuel infrastructure is needed!!

- Incentives are needed to provide the American Auto Co's the necessary motivation to invest in PHEV's

- American People and government need to experience real demonstration vehicles built by professional staff to Show real **Personal Energy Independence is achievable!!**

tion NOW!!

Solar and other renewable

 fuels can begin our transition

sumption.

ow us to integrate our

and stationary energy systems

r efficiency thus reducing our

on energy consumption.

d of vehicle for energy security,
**improved** society.

ublic demand for these cars &
atures possible from these large

ct the first 1500 or more
hicles to provide the public,
industry with a fleet of vehicles

Mr. ISSA. David, are you roughly 5 minutes?

Mr. HERMANCE. Yes, sir.

Mr. ISSA. We will do your testimony, and I will run like a bunny for two votes, one which should be just about over and the next, and then I will return. They are the last votes of the day, and I am yours when I get back.

### STATEMENT OF DAVID HERMANCE

Mr. HERMANCE. Mr. Chairman and members of the committee, my name is Dave Hermance; and I'm the executive engineer for Advanced Technology Vehicles at Toyota's Technical Center in Los Angeles. I want to thank you for inviting Toyota to participate in this hearing and to provide our perspective on hybrid vehicles.

Toyota believes that there is no single fuel or powertrain technology that can solve all of society's transportation needs. Simply put, there is no silver bullet. This is why Toyota and many other companies are pursuing multiple fuel and technology paths in the continuing quest to reduce the impact of the automobile on society.

Through our research, we have discovered one key, however, to making improving efficiency of any choice of fuel or powertrain system and that is hybridization. Toyota is committed to hybrid as a core technology for future product.

Today, by combining a secondary energy storage system, usually a battery, with conventional powertrains, Toyota's hybrid energy drive has the ability to reduce fuel consumption, reduce criteria pollutants and increase the "fun to drive" of the vehicle, which is why some people drive.

In the future, similar hybrid systems can be combined with new diesel technology or alternative fuels technology or, ultimately, maybe even with hydrogen fuel cell technology. In all of those cases, hybridization increases the efficiency of any fuel or powertrain system; and increased efficiency is what is going to be the key to admission to the future.

The vehicle purchase process is usually not an academic exercise in logic. It is usually more an emotional process. Manufacturers strive to find a balance of attributes that a potential customer will value. The overall process is referred to as finding the right value proposition, and this will likely vary by market segment, and it may vary over time, depending on what fuel prices and other outside effects are in play.

For example, the Prius pairs a best-in-class fuel economy, saving about 350 gallons of fuel per year relative to class average, with class average acceleration performance. The Lexus GS 450h provides better than V–8 performance, while saving about 160 gallons of fuel per year. And the new Camry hybrid vehicle offers better performance than many midsize V–6 products, while saving about 220 gallons of fuel per year.

I should note that all Toyota and Lexus hybrid vehicles are federally certified as Tier 2—Bin 3 and in California as superultra low emission vehicles. Importantly, hybrid vehicles are saving fuel today using the existing infrastructure.

Since our introduction of Prius in the Japan market in 1997, Toyota's cumulative global hybrid sales have exceeded 600,000 units. Of that total, slightly more than 300,000 through the end of the first quarter have been in the United States. We have sold another 50,000 since then in the States.

Currently, Toyota has five hybrid models on sale in the United States and one additional model, the Lexus LS 600h, which you can buy——

Mr. ISSA. Which I have on order.

Mr. HERMANCE. All right—in 2007 as a 2008 model year vehicle. Clearly, the United States is an important market for Toyota's hybrid strategy.

Moving forward, we can easily see the results of Toyota's continuous improvement philosophy by examining the improvements in Prius over the initial 6 years since it was launched. Since launch, we have increased the combined label fuel economy by over 30 percent, we have improved the acceleration performance from zero to 60 by 4.4 seconds, and we have steadily reduced the already low emissions. These enhancements are the result of increasing the efficiency of all the components, steady improvements in battery technology, and applied learning to the control systems. Over the same time interval, the vehicle has also grown physically in size to better meet the U.S. market and sold at steadily higher volumes, and we also managed to take 50 percent of the cost out of the component set.

As a direct result of this approach, we can foresee a time when we offer a hybrid in every segment in which we compete. Over time, the cost/benefit of our hybrid systems will be improved to the point that a hybrid becomes a normal "check the box" option for a powertrain, just like a choice of a 4, 6 or 8 cylinder engine is today. Our goal is to double the number of hybrid models by early next decade, and it is reasonable to expect that doing so will bring Toyota's global hybrid production to over a million units a year. We also plan to take 50 percent of the cost out of the system in that time interval as well.

Thank you, Mr. Chairman. I will be happy to answer your questions now or later.

Mr. ISSA. I am going to depart for just a few moments.

[The prepared statement of Mr. Hermance follows:]

60

Toyota Testimony

By Dave Hermance

Executive Engineer for Advanced Technology Vehicles

On

"Hybrid Cars:  Increasing Fuel Efficiency and

Reducing Oil Dependence"

Before the

House Government Reform Subcommittee on Energy Resources

July 20, 2006

embers of the committee, my name is D

eer for Advanced Technology Vehicles a

es. I want to thank you for inviting Toyota

de our perspective on hybrid vehicles.

there is no single fuel or powertrain tech

transportation needs.  Simply put, there

s pursuing multiple fuel and technology p

educe the impact of the automobile on s

a secondary energy storage system wit

's Hybrid Synergy Drive system has the

e criteria pollutants and increase the "fur

## *ential Hybrid Benefi*

### uced Fuel Consumption
wer operating cost, less $CO_2$, less oil consun

### uced Exhaust Emissions
tter air quality, reduced adverse health effec

### e Fun to drive
uicker 0-60, better passing, less cabin noise,
od"

### binations of the Above

e process is usually not an academic exe

e to find a balance of attributes that a pote

process is referred to as finding the right

ry by segment and perhaps over time.

*rid Value Propositior*

facturers strive to find the combination of
ding hybrid attributes) that customers valu
illing to pay for

kely that this combination will vary by mod
nly will vary by segment

w models are introduced this balance ma
ge and it may evolve over time as market
ge

the vehicle purchase process is more tha
emic exercise in logic, we look at more tha
to recover cost or acceleration performar

on of Prius in 1997, Toyota's cumulative

,000 units.  Of this total, over 300,000 ha

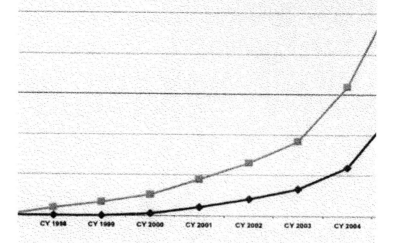

*mulative Toyota Hybr*
*es*

- Cumulative Global
- Cumulative US

CY 1998    CY 1999    CY 2000    CY 2001    CY 2002    CY 2003    CY 2004

as five different hybrid models on sale in

can easily see the results of Toyota's co

phy by examining the improvements in F

launched.

## s History

| ars | 1998-2000 * | 2001-2003 | |
|---|---|---|---|
| FE | 43 | 52 | |
| Label FE | 41 | 45 | |
| d Label FE | 42 | 48 | |
| el | 14.5 | 12.5 | |
| s | LEV | SULEV | A |
| s | Subcompact | Compact | |
| | Minor Model Change | Model Change | |
| me | * Japan only | ~50,000/3 yr | ~5 |
| | | | 108, |

oved to the point that a hybrid becomes

on, just like four, six and eight cylinders

iber of hybrid models by early in the next

to expect that doing so could bring Toyo

million units annually.  We also plan to t

of the system.

## bal Toyota Goals

cost reduction by 2004 Model
00 hybrids total by 2005
00 per year rate by mid-decade

ional 50% cost reduction by early nex
,000 per year rate by early next decad

Mr. Issa. I have to be honest, Mr. Hermance. I have had nothing but Toyota and Lexus hybrids, but I am looking forward to seeing what Honda has to offer. It is just an order. It is cancelable still. So this is a perfect segue for me to depart for a moment and Honda to think about the hard sale.

With that, we will stand in recess for about 20 minutes.

[Recess.]

Mr. Issa. Thank you all for your patience.

As earlier promised, before we begin again, the ranking member, the gentlewoman from California, Ms. Watson, will make her opening statement.

Ms. Watson. Thank you, Mr. Chairman.

Because our Nation's demand for energy has increased 30 percent since 1990 and the U.S. Energy Information Administration estimates that the demand will rise another 45 percent by 2025, it is important for us to be researching and examining all possible solutions to our energy problem. The purpose of this hearing is to examine the innovative technology of hybrid vehicles and assess what the potential for hybrid vehicles is in increasing the overall fuel efficiency of automobiles while decreasing our dependence on imported oil.

There are several potential benefits to increasing the number of hybrid vehicles on America's roads, but do those benefits outweigh the costs of possibly having more cars on the road, increasing congestion? Is this breakthrough technology the answer to our environmental problems with fuel emissions? And I hope that our witnesses will address that. I know that you have started; and so, if you have given us that information, maybe you can put it in writing to my office.

Hybrid vehicles are becoming increasingly popular in the United States compared to the traditional vehicles. Hybrids are more fuel efficient, emit lower amounts of fuel, and their use in the long run is less expensive. The United States saw the sale of its first hybrid in 1999 and went from only 10,000 vehicles sold in 2000 to almost 206,000 sold in 2005. They have many cost savings, State taxes and environmental benefits.

In my own State of California where the traffic problems are among the worst in the Nation, there are several benefits for purchasers of hybrid vehicles. An example, if you own a zero emission vehicle or a superultra low emission vehicle in the city of Los Angeles, you can park without paying at metered parking spaces throughout our city. Other States have adopted tax incentives for consumers who purchase alternative fuel and advanced technology vehicles.

These incentives are great, but are they really helping us accomplish our goal of saving energy and taking cars off the road? Saving energy is everyone's responsibility. Almost every aspect of business and commerce use some type of energy to perform their daily operations. Automakers especially need to work with government to set reasonable goals to improve fuel economy standards and reduce greenhouse gasses.

So, Mr. Chairman, it is important that, while we do want to advance the production of hybrid vehicles, we do take into account that we should caution against simply promoting hybrid technology as the answer to promoting fuel efficiency and reducing oil dependence. We must explore what we can do to focus on a broad range of policies that would transition toward the use of renewable resources, reduce emission of greenhouse gasses and other air toxins and promote a reduction in driving habits. We need to work with the industry experts in developing policies that would include stronger fuel economy standards, which would benefit both the hybrid industry and our environment.

Again, I thank our witnesses for your input; and I thank you, Mr. Chairman, for calling this meeting. I look forward to the testimony, and I yield back.

Mr. ISSA. Thank you.

Mr. German, you have been very patient. The floor is yours.

## STATEMENT OF JOHN GERMAN

Mr. GERMAN. Thank you, Mr. Chairman. I welcome the break so perhaps you will not realize how similar my first two paragraphs are to Mr. Hermance's.

Mr. ISSA. As we said before the break, it is the difference in cars we want to hear about. It is very similar of the Toyota Prius' determination of whether or not its passive start works. Up is on and down is off.

Mr. GERMAN. Good morning, Mr. Chairman and members of the subcommittee. My name is John German, and I am manager of environmental and energy analysis for the American Honda Motor Co. Let me thank you for the opportunity to provide Honda's views on the subject of hybrid vehicles and their role in the Nation's efforts to reduce its consumption of petroleum.

Hybrid technology offers very significant opportunities for improving vehicle fuel economy, and that is one of the reasons why Honda was an early adopter of the technology. It is important to point out, however, that global demand for transportation energy is so immense that no single technology can possibly be the solution. There is no magic bullet. We are going to need rapid development and implementation of as many feasible technologies as possible.

Honda has a long history of being a technology and efficiency leader. Our overall philosophy is to be a company that society wants to exist. One of the results of this philosophy is Honda's leadership on hybrid vehicle development.

We introduced the first hybrid vehicle in the United States in 1999, the Honda Insight. This vehicle was designed to showcase the potential of hybrids and advanced technology. The Civic Hybrid, introduced in 2002, was the first hybrid powertrain offered as an option on a mainstream model. The Accord Hybrid was the first V6 hybrid, and the 2006 Civic Hybrid incorporated significant improvements to the battery, electric motor and hybrid operating system to improve both efficiency and performance.

Honda's commitment to reduce energy consumption extends beyond hybrid vehicles. As the world's largest producer of internal combustion engines, we have already incorporated many technologies to make those engines more efficient, and there is substantially more that can be done in the future. For example, Honda pioneered variable valve timing in the early 1990's, and we now use it on 100 percent of our vehicles.

For the future, we have announced plans to introduce within the next 2 years a more advanced version of Honda's four-cylinder i-VTEC technology with up to a 13 percent improvement in fuel efficiency over 2005 levels and a more advanced variable cylinder management technology for six-cylinder engines with up to an 11 percent improvement in fuel efficiency.

Honda has also announced its intention to introduce within 3 years a clean diesel vehicle, meeting stringent clean air standards and achieving up to 30 percent better fuel economy.

Honda also believes that alternative fuels offer significant potential. We are the only company that continues to offer a dedicated compressed natural gas vehicle, the third generation Civic GX.

We recently introduced a home natural gas refueling station that will expand the market beyond fleets to retail customers. We were the first company to certify a fuel cell vehicle with the EPA and the first to lease a fuel cell vehicle to an individual customer.

So development of hybrid vehicles needs to be viewed within this context. Hybrids have a lot of potential, but to achieve significant market penetration they must be able to compete in terms of cost, performance and utility with advanced gasoline and diesel engines. In this regard, the most important factor to consider is to reduce the cost, size and weight of the battery pack. We have found that today's hybrid customers are most interested in fuel cost savings, but at this juncture mainstream consumers do not value the fuel savings as highly and hybrid sales represent only about 1 percent of annual sales nationwide. Market penetration will increase as the costs come down in the future.

Taking what we have learned, Honda's next step in hybrid vehicle development will be the introduction of an all-new hybrid car to be launched in North America in 2006. The hybrid vehicle will be a dedicated, hybrid-only model with a target price lower than that of the current Civic Hybrid. I am not sure it is a direct competitor to the LS 600h, but I can check it out. We are targeting an annual North American sales volume of 100,000 units, mostly in the United States, and 200,000 sales worldwide.

The ability for hybrids to reduce refuel consumption and green house gas emissions is proportional to the efficiency improvements and market share. If hybrids increase to a 5 percent market share, this will reduce in-use fuel consumption and $CO_2$ emissions by 1 to 2 percent. A 10-percent market share will offer 2 to 4 percent reductions. Note that there is nothing distinctive to hybrids about these effects. The same benefit could be obtained by raising the overall fleet fuel economy using conventional gasoline technology or diesel engines.

As Honda has previously announced, we believe it is time for the Federal Government to take action to improve vehicle economy. Performance requirements and incentives are the most effective policy instruments, as they allow manufacturers to develop and implement the most cost-effective solutions. One example would be to increase the CAFE standards. The NHTSA already has the authority to regulate vehicle efficiency, and Honda has called upon the agency to increase the stringency of the fuel economy requirements, and we have also supported efforts to reform the passenger car standards. At the same time, Congress should develop a program of broad, performance-based incentives to stimulate demand in the marketplace to purchase vehicles that meet the new requirements.

The other effective action the government can take is research into improved energy storage. The success of the electric drive technologies, including hybrids and fuel cells, depends on our ability to build less expensive, lighter and more robust energy storage devices.

The Department of Energy's work in this area should be supported and funded by Congress.

I appreciate the opportunity to present Honda's views, and I would be happy to address any questions you have.

Mr. ISSA. Thank you.

[The prepared statement of Mr. German follows:]

Statement of John German, Manager
Environmental and Energy Analysis
Product Regulatory Office
American Honda Motor Company, Inc.
Before the
House Government Reform Subcommittee on Energy and Resources

U.S. House of Representatives
July 20, 2006

Good morning Mr. Chairman and members of the Subcommittee. My name is John German and I am Manager of Environmental and Energy Analysis with American Honda Motor Company. We thank you for the opportunity to provide Honda's views on the subject of hybrid vehicles and their role in the nation's efforts to reduce its consumption of petroleum.

Hybrid technology offers very significant opportunities for improving vehicle fuel economy and that is one of the reasons why Honda was an early adopter of the technology. It is important to point out, however, that global demand for transportation energy is so immense that no single technology can possibly be the solution. There is no magic bullet – we are going to need rapid development and implementation of as many feasible technologies as possible.

Honda has a long history of being a technology and efficiency leader. Our overall philosophy is to be a company that society wants to exist. One of the results of this philosophy is Honda's leadership on hybrid vehicle development. We introduced the first hybrid vehicle in the US in 1999, the Honda Insight. This vehicle was designed to showcase the potential of hybrids and advanced technology. The Civic Hybrid, introduced in 2002, was the first hybrid powertrain offered as an option on a mainstream model. The Accord Hybrid was the first V6 hybrid. The 2006 Civic Hybrid incorporated significant improvements to the battery, electric motor, and hybrid operating strategy to improve both efficiency and performance.

Honda's commitment to reduce energy consumption extends beyond hybrid vehicles. As the world's biggest producer of internal combustion engines, there is much that has already been done to make those engines more efficient and substantially more that can be done in the future. For example, Honda pioneered variable valve timing in the early 1990s and we now use it on 100% of our vehicles. Similarly, virtually all of our engines are aluminum block with overhead camshafts and 4-valves per cylinder; and all of our transmissions have at least five speeds. All of these technologies are making our vehicles more fuel efficient. For the future, Honda has announced plans to introduce within the next two years a more advanced version of Honda's four-cylinder i-VTEC technology with up to a 13 percent improvement in fuel efficiency over 2005 levels, and a more advanced Variable Cylinder Management (VCM) technology for six-cylinder engines with up to an 11 percent improvement in fuel efficiency. Honda also has announced its intention to introduce within three years a clean diesel vehicle, meeting stringent clean air standards and achieving up to 30% better fuel economy.

Honda also believes that alternative fuels offer significant potential. We are the only company that continues to offer a dedicated compressed natural gas vehicle, the third generation Civic GX.

We recently introduced a home natural gas refueling station that will expand the market beyond fleets to retail customers. We were the first company to certify a fuel cell vehicle with the EPA and the first to lease a fuel cell vehicle to an individual customer.

Development of hybrid vehicles needs to be viewed within this context. Hybrids have a lot of potential, but to achieve significant market penetration they must be able to compete, in terms of cost, performance and utility, with advanced gasoline and diesel engines. In this regard, the most important factor is to continue to reduce the cost, size, and weight of the battery pack. We have found that today's hybrid customers are most interested in fuel cost savings. But at this juncture, mainstream customers do not value the fuel savings as highly and hybrid sales represent only about 1% of annual sales. Market penetration will increase as the costs are reduced in the future.

Taking what we have learned, Honda's next step in hybrid vehicle development will be the introduction of an all-new hybrid car to be launched in North America in 2009. This new hybrid vehicle will be a dedicated, hybrid-only model with a target price lower than that of the current Civic Hybrid. We are targeting an annual North American sales volume of 100,000 units, mostly in the United States, and 200,000 units worldwide.

As you know, Mr. Chairman, Congress has enacted a program of consumer incentives to encourage the purchase of hybrid vehicles. We believe the current incentive program is flawed in two respects. First and foremost, there should be a change in the metric used to calculate the value of the credit that would more accurately reflect how the vehicles are actually being operated. Currently, the incentives are calculated using a city only fuel economy metric. Honda suggests a change to a combined (city/highway) metric. Most drivers use their vehicles for both city and highway driving and the incentive metric should reflect that reality. In addition, the 60,000 per manufacturer vehicle cap should be replaced. It creates market distortions which benefit manufacturers who have not sold their quota of vehicles or who have been slow to enter the market. If Congress is going to maintain an incentive program, it should consider one in which the customers of all manufacturers have the same access to the incentive program at the same time. For example, the current program could be replaced with a three-year incentive program with 100% of the value of the credit available in 2007, 50% in 2008 and 25% in 2009. The incentive would sunset in 2010.

The ability for hybrids to reduce fuel consumption and greenhouse gas emissions is proportional to the efficiency improvements and market share. If hybrids increase to 5% market share, this will reduce in-use fuel consumption and $CO_2$ emissions by 1-2%. A 10% market share will offer 2-4% reductions. Note that there is nothing distinctive to hybrids about these effects. The same benefit could be obtained by raising the overall fleet fuel economy using conventional gasoline technology or introducing diesel engines.

I also want to address the issue of ethanol. There is an important role for ethanol in reducing U.S. consumption of petroleum. Some are suggesting that we use the ethanol we currently are producing to make a fuel that is 85% ethanol (called "E-85"). The problem with that approach is that vehicles have to be specially engineered to run on E-85. E-85 also requires a separate distribution system and separate pumps. The cost of installing pumps alone is in the tens of thousands of dollars per station. Also unknown is whether customers will accept 25% lower fuel economy with E-85 and more frequent trips to the gas station. We believe that instead of using our ethanol to create E-85 fuels, it should instead be blended with gasoline at up to 10% levels ("E-10"). Unlike E-85, E-10 does not require a whole new infrastructure and vehicles already on the road can operate safely on E-10. The nation's objective of reducing petroleum consumption by using ethanol can be more efficiently and effectively achieved with E-10 rather than E-85.

As Honda has previously announced, we believe it is time for the Federal government to take action to improve vehicle economy. Performance requirements and incentives are the most effective policy instruments, as they allow manufacturers to develop and implement the most cost-effective solutions. One example would be to increase the CAFE standards. The NHTSA already has the authority to regulate vehicle efficiency and Honda has called upon the agency to increase the stringency of the fuel economy requirements and has supported efforts to reform the passenger car standards. At the same time, Congress should develop a program of broad, performance-based incentives to stimulate demand in the marketplace to purchase vehicles that meet the new requirements.

The other effective action the government can take is research into improved energy storage. The success of electric drive technologies, including hybrids and fuel cells, depends on our ability to build less expensive, lighter and more robust energy storage devices. The Department of Energy's work in this area should be supported and funded by Congress.

I appreciate the opportunity to present Honda's views and would be happy to address any questions you may have.

Mr. ISSA. Mr. MacKenzie.

## STATEMENT OF DON MACKENZIE

Mr. MACKENZIE. Thank you, Mr. Chairman and Chairwoman for the opportunity to testify before you today. I'm an engineer in the clean vehicles program at the Union of Concerned Scientists, a national nonprofit alliance of citizens and scientists who have been working at the intersection of science and policy for over 30 years. We also maintain a now award-winning Web site, hybridcenter.org, that is dedicated to educating the public on hybrid vehicles.

Hybrids are indeed a timely subject. Despite the nay-saying from some and the reneging of certain automakers on their hybrid commitments, the hybrid market as a whole continues to grow quickly. In fact, hybrid sales in the second quarter of this year were up 20 percent over the same period last year. That said, hybrids still represent only a quarter of a percent of all the vehicles on our roads and continue to need support if they are going to live up to their potential.

They do have a significant potential to help reduce our dependence on oil and the environmental and economic burdens that come with that dependence. But hybrids alone cannot deliver the kind of reductions that we need. To solve our oil dependence problem, we need a three-pronged approach that will: No. 1, reduce the amount of fuel that consumers burn by increasing fuel economy standards for all vehicles. This is an area where hybrids can help. No. 2, we need to reduce the number of miles that our vehicles are being driven. And No. 3, in the long term we need to replace the petroleum fuels that we're still using with sustainable low-carbon alternatives.

A good advanced technology hybrid is capable of doubling fuel economy and can be equipped to use alternative fuels, but not all hybrids are created equal. Those like the Toyota Prius, Honda Civic hybrid, the Escape hybrid and now the Camry hybrid increase fuel economy by 40 to 80 percent. On the other hand, muscle hybrids like Honda's Accord and the Lexus GS–450h from Toyota forego fuel savings in favor of faster acceleration, thus missing out on much of the potential of hybrid technology. Hollow hybrids like GM's Silverado pickup claim the hybrid name, but don't have the true hybrid's ability to capture and reuse significant quantities of energy.

A further challenge is that if the sale of a hybrid is offset by the sale of another gas guzzler, then there is no net savings in oil use. Despite leading the industry in hybrid sales, both Toyota's and Honda's overall average fuel economy is projected to be lower in 2006 than in 2005, this is according to an EPA report that was released this week. It is therefore somewhat inaccurate to ascribe specific fuel savings numbers to hybrid sales to date. The way to ensure that the U.S. car and truck fleet cuts down on its oil use is through increases in fuel economy standards.

I will now discuss some steps that the Federal Government can take to encourage greater sales of clean, high-fuel-economy hybrids, and ensure these hybrids deliver the maximum possible benefit in terms of reduced oil use. Any incentives for hybrids should be designed to encourage the sale of vehicles that take full advantage of the technology's potential for increasing fuel economy. Putting aside all jargon and classifications, the bottom line is how much of a fuel economy increase does this vehicle deliver and how much pollution comes out of the tailpipe.

The structure of the Federal hybrid tax credit is a good example of a rational, performance-based incentive that gives larger credits to hybrids that deliver larger fuel economy gains. The fatal flaw in this program is the 60,000-vehicle-per-manufacturer cap on the number of eligible vehicles, which will soon take away credits from many of the best hybrid models while leaving credits in place for poor performers. Congress should make it a priority to lift this cap as quickly as it can.

Members of the committee and others in Congress have identified the importance of producing hybrid vehicles and their components in the United States. Congress should adopt manufacturing incentives that promote the production of hybrid technologies in the United States, but should do so only if these incentives are linked to increases in fuel economy. This pairing avoids corporate welfare, and ensuring that meaningful increases in fleet fuel economy are achieved. Industry should not receive public dollars unless a public benefit is guaranteed in return.

Manufacturing incentives tied to increased fuel economy are essential because it is high gas prices and not investments in technology that threaten domestic auto manufacturing. A study by the University of Michigan and the Natural Resources Defense Council found that as a result of the Big Three's poor positioning on fuel economy and technology, a sustained gas price of $2.86 a gallon would put almost 300,000 Americans out of work. In contrast, a study by UCS found that increasing fuel economy standards to 40 mpg over 10 years would lead to the creation of 160,000 new jobs nationwide, including 40,000 in the automotive sector.

I will stop there, and I thank you for the opportunity to testify, and I look forward to your questions.

Mr. ISSA. Thank you. And thank you very much for observing the 5 minutes. That is always very much appreciated.

[The prepared statement of Mr. MacKenzie follows:]

STATEMENT OF:
## THE UNION OF CONCERNED SCIENTISTS

BEFORE THE:
## HOUSE COMMITTEE ON GOVERNMENT REFORM
## SUBCOMMITTEE ON ENERGY AND RESOURCES

PRESENTED BY
## DON MacKENZIE
## VEHICLES ENGINEER

## JULY 19, 2006

Thank you Mr. Chairman and Members of the Committee for the opportunity to testify before you today. I am an engineer in the Union of Concerned Scientists' (UCS) Clean Vehicles Program. UCS is a nonprofit partnership of scientists and citizens that has been working at the intersection of science and policy for over 30 years, and maintains the award winning website, HybridCenter.org, dedicated to educating the public on hybrid vehicles.

Hybrids are indeed a timely subject. Despite the naysaying from some and the reneging of certain automakers on commitments to produce more hybrids, the hybrid market as a whole continues to grow apace. Hybrid sales in the second quarter of 2006 were up 20% compared to the same period last year. That said, however, hybrids represent only one quarter of one percent of all the cars and trucks on the road and continue to need support if they are to live up to their potential.

Hybrids have significant potential to help reduce America's dependence on oil, lessen the impact of near record high gasoline prices, and address the automobile's impact on climate change. However, they are just part of the first step needed to reduce the impacts of our dependence on oil. Alone, hybrids will not deliver the kind of reductions that we need. To solve this problem, we need a three-pronged approach that will:

1. Reduce the amount of fuel consumers burn by increasing fuel economy standards,
2. Reduce the number of miles that our vehicles are being driven, and
3. In the long term, replace the petroleum fuels that we are using with sustainable, low-carbon alternatives.

A good, advanced technology hybrid is capable of doubling fuel economy and can be equipped to use alternative fuels. However, not all hybrids are created equal. Hybrids like the Toyota Prius, Honda Civic Hybrid, Ford Escape Hybrid and the new Toyota Camry hybrid increase fuel economy by 40-80%. On the other hand, muscle hybrids like the Honda Accord and Toyota's Lexus GS 450h forego fuel savings in favor of faster acceleration, missing out on the potential savings of the technology. Hollow hybrids like GM's Silverado pickup claim the hybrid name but do not have the true hybrid's ability to capture and reuse significant quantities of energy.

A further challenge is that if the sale of a hybrid merely offsets the sale of another gas guzzler, then there is no net savings in oil use. Despite leading the industry in hybrid sales, both Toyota's and Honda's overall average fuel economy is projected to be lower in 2006 than in 2005, according to an EPA report released this week.[1] It is therefore inaccurate to attribute any specific fuel savings numbers to hybrid sales to date. The way to ensure that the US car and truck fleet cuts down on its oil use is through increases in fuel economy standards.

I will now discuss some steps that the federal government can take to encourage greater sales of clean, high fuel economy hybrid vehicles, and to ensure that these hybrids deliver the maximum possible benefit in terms of reducing oil use.

Any incentives for hybrid vehicles should be designed to encourage the sale of hybrids that take full advantage of the technology's potential for increasing fuel economy. All jargon and classifications aside, the bottom line is, "How much of a fuel economy increase does this vehicle deliver, and how much pollution comes out of the tailpipe?" The structure of the federal hybrid tax credit is an excellent example of a rational, performance-based incentive that gives larger credits to hybrids that deliver larger fuel economy gains. The fatal flaw in this program is the 60,000 vehicle per manufacturer cap on the number of eligible vehicles, which will soon take away credits for some of the best hybrids on the market, while leaving credits for many poor performers. Congress should make it a priority to lift this cap as quickly as possible.

Members of the committee and others in Congress have identified the importance of producing hybrid vehicles and their components in the United States. Congress should adopt manufacturing incentives that promote the production of hybrid technologies in the US, but only if they are directly linked to increases in fuel economy standards. This pairing avoids corporate welfare and ensures that meaningful increases in fleet fuel economy are achieved. Industry should not receive public dollars unless a public benefit is guaranteed in return.

Manufacturing incentives tied to increased fuel economy are essential because it is high gas prices, and not investments in technology, that threaten domestic auto manufacturing. A study by the University of Michigan and the NRDC found that as a result of the Big Three's poor positioning on fuel economy and technology, a sustained gas price of $2.86 per gallon would put almost 300,000 Americans out of work. In contrast, a study by the Union of Concerned Scientists found that increasing fuel economy standards to 40 MPG by 2015 would lead to the creation of 160,000 new jobs nationwide, including 40,000 in the automotive sector.

Finally, I would also like to address one policy which has been successful in stimulating hybrid sales, but whose time has now passed. Hybrid HOV programs have allowed drivers of hybrid vehicles to drive in high-occupancy vehicle lanes without any passengers. In areas with congested freeways like California and Northern Virginia, this has proven to be a significant incentive. Unfortunately, such programs have inevitably fallen victim to their own success. As the number of hybrid vehicles grows, HOV lanes become more crowded, eventually to the point where their primary function – to reduce congestion and encourage carpooling – is impaired. It is time for governments to focus on other incentives that will stimulate continued growth of hybrid

---

[1] Heavenrich, Robert M. *Light-Duty Automotive Technology and Fuel Economy Trends: 1975 through 2006* EPA420-R-06-011, July 2006.

sales without forcing air quality or other tradeoffs. It is also far past time for the federal government to significantly raise fuel economy standards for all cars and trucks to ensure that all consumers, not just hybrid buyers, can find relief from the high cost of driving.

Thank you again for the opportunity to testify today. I would be happy to answer any questions you may have.

Mr. Issa. We will get right to questions. I will lead off.

First of all, Mr. German, I will look at the 2006 Civic for my son. Having said that, I would like to start with Mr. MacKenzie.

The EPA report on Honda, if I understand correctly, the projected reduction has to do with the mix that Honda is enjoying primarily because the Big Three have dominated the full-size truck market for a long time, and Honda and Toyota and others are now going into that. This is a mixed change, not a "per a given like vehicle" reduction. In other words, the Honda Accord is not going down in mileage, the Honda Civic is not going down. No major platform is going down in mileage, but rather the projected mix is anticipated to be different. Is that roughly what I remember reading?

Mr. MacKenzie. Yes, that's a very good point, and I think it illustrates the need for us to have increases in fuel economy standards at the same time as we have incentives for some of these high-fuel-economy vehicles in order to ensure that we get those increases.

Mr. Issa. This goes back to a question I have specifically for you because you touched on this. I am a supporter of CAFE standard increases. I am personally convinced that we should never have stops and starts that send mixed messages to the industry. They can be incredibly small if technology is sort of at a stumbling point and larger if we see opportunities.

Having said that, don't you agree, or would you be willing to agree with me, that a modernized CAFE should look at each category, where we expect them to be, where they can be, and begin increases in fuel economy by major categories? Meaning if I have a family of one grown child, so by definition my wife and I drive alone, but if you have seven children and you need to carry nine people, that realistically you don't have the option of going to the Honda Civic, you have to choose a family sedan or perhaps even a van of some sort.

So wouldn't you agree that, in fact, CAFE standards should observe block categories, although we could disagree on where those blocks are; that the ratings should be on some tangible performance that is unique to perhaps a slightly larger vehicle.

Mr. MacKenzie. I think the idea of a class-based or attribute-based standard is reasonable. If you look at the rule that NHTSA came out with for trucks, that does a good job of addressing a lot of the concerns about possible disparate impacts on different manufacturers. What we need now is to see larger increases, see that kind of a framework, but using that to drive larger increases that we know are possible with the technology that is available.

Mr. Issa. And then I don't want to dwell on CAFE, but for both of the auto manufacturers, realistically I would assume that your companies, as representatives of many companies, support that concept; that you can look at each of your major platform categories and work to improve standards on a platform-by-platform basis. Is this a reasonable approach as you view it?

Mr. German. Honda has supported CAFE increases. We are on record that we actually prefer the current system, but that if you do want to do an attribute system, that size works a lot better than weight. We are happy that NHTSA adopted a size system, and we are supportive of the system.

Mr. ISSA. And I was referring to a size system. I don't want to penalize something for using aluminum rather than steel.

Mr. GERMAN. Exactly.

Mr. ISSA. Moving back into the core, as we talked about batteries, because part of this hearing is how much further can we go, supercapacitors typically, as well as capacitor-type technology, typically intake and outflow capacity of electricity quicker and can operate at higher voltage. Would you recommend that when the Federal Government is looking at these developments that we look specifically to higher voltages so that you can have more efficient electric motors and the coupling of those? Does that make sense?

I will give Dr. Frank a chance. In a plug-in environment this may not always be optimal, but certainly when you are looking at quick recovery for some kinetic energy savings? Doctor.

Mr. FRANK. Ultracapacitors have higher efficiency and higher power capability, but when you go to a plug-in hybrid where you have a lot of batteries, you already have high power capacity, so you don't need ultracapacity. The only purpose of ultracapacity is you want to stick to a very small battery pack, but if you stick to a small battery pack, you can't make a plug-in. The big battery pack does everything that the ultracapacitor will do, but better.

Mr. ISSA. I appreciate that.

I noted that the some of the studies have suggested that it is a hybrid of the hybrid, if you will, that mixing batteries for depth and capacitors for those quick on and off accelerators may also be part. Are these the nuances that we should be looking at?

Mr. HERMANCE. You can indeed increase overall efficiency, particularly on the regenaritive side, with the use of ultracapacitors, but they store very little energy. So even in today's hybrids, not even toward plug-in hybrids, you're marginal whether you can store enough energy in a capacitor. So, yes, those applications that have used both have generally used them together, with the exception of some fuel cell applications which are quite different applications.

The bus industry has used both combinations of battery storage and capacitor storage, and that is possible. The one downside is that capacitors are both pricey, and they take a lot of volume.

Mr. ISSA. But they are light.

Mr. HERMANCE. No, they are actually not. Well, they are light for their unit volume, but they are not free from a weight standpoint.

Mr. ISSA. Of course.

Mr. HERMANCE. But they are also quite expensive, and you have to balance the benefit you might get from that improvement with the cost of that system and whether that makes a viable decision for the customer.

Mr. GERMAN. Right now Honda is using ultracapacitor on our fuel cell vehicle where you don't need much energy storage. But I agree with all the comments of Dr. Frank and Dave Hermance. The only thing I will add is that there is some very early stage research being done on using nanotubes with ultracapacitors, which has the potential, if it works out, to tremendously increase the storage capacity and still maintain all the good characteristics. It is a long way off, but it is fun to watch this stuff.

Mr. ISSA. When I was a young boy in the auto industry, we generally looked at about 32 volts. As we got above that, we started worrying about arcing, we started worrying about all the disadvantages that keep us from putting our finger anywhere near 110 volts if it were DC. However, in the technology that you are both going toward, clearly voltage matters, and you are going up in voltage.

Where is the sweet spot now and in the long run in voltage development? In other words, how high can you go in order to reduce the size of the electric motor and gain other efficiencies? And where are your engineering challenges today that the government might play a role in helping to get past?

Mr. HERMANCE. You want to go first, John?

Mr. GERMAN. No.

Mr. HERMANCE. OK. Today our systems operate at as high a voltage as 650 volts. There is a practical limit that changes to a different class of materials if you go much beyond that. There is a little more margin, but not a lot more. The other break point that you mentioned before is at nominally 50-volt system. Below that there are different requirements for safety. At high voltage you require a level of safety, isolation and what-not that is different from the low-voltage systems. But there are practical limits to the voltage as well from the standpoint of the class of materials that you use to provide the necessary isolation, and it is not a lot higher than the 650 that is in current use.

Mr. ISSA. So you think your voltage is getting close to where it can be? And by definition does that mean that you are going to multiple motors, which I know is in Toyota's strategy, but multiple motors is going to become a bigger strategy?

Mr. HERMANCE. Actually, you don't need to go to multiple motors. You might go to an additional motor for all-wheel drive, which allows you a little bit better regen capture, but at a cost. We are managing to make the motors themselves more compact over time. Really we don't see a need to go to multiple motors from a traction power standpoint. We just made them more efficient and more compact by going to the higher voltage.

Mr. GERMAN. Having electric motors in each wheel is an interesting idea which has a number of efficiencies. The problem is that is unsprung mass; that is, mass that has to be controlled by the springs and affects ride and handling of the vehicle. So far we haven't figured out how to make electric motors light enough to be able to put them in the wheels.

Mr. ISSA. You can put them in the middle of the transaxle. Sadly enough, I had an Indy car team, and we never solved the problem of our unsprung weight versus the competitors', so we never won in my years.

I am going to finish up here. I guess I will ask for a second round, but when I look at California's experiment with the zero emissions vehicle, the General Motors famous leased vehicle, an abysmal failure because it was, in fact, a product that needed special charging, and it basically had limited range, and then you had to find yourself a high-voltage source and plug in and wait.

82

Dr. Frank, particularly for the technology you are looking at, I see that essentially what you are hoping to get by is to find the sweet spot of 60 or so miles so that we can avoid the problems of the General Motors vehicle and incorporate the ability beyond 60 miles to go from plugged, if you will, to totally unplugged. Is that roughly the basis for your preference toward a plugged hybrid?

Mr. FRANK. That's exactly the objective. But the plug-in hybrid opens the door to renewable energy use directly as well. So the plug-in hybrid solves all the problems of the pure electric vehicle because there is no charging infrastructure. You have always got gasoline on board. It is a dual-energy-source system. So because of the dual-energy-source capability, you don't have to charge quickly, and that's one of the main features, so that means you can charge with conventional 120-volt plugs, which are everywhere in our society already.

Mr. ISSA. Last question, Mr. Hermance. I'm going to put you on the spot and use the bloggers against you. You are probably familiar with the Prius stealth mode modifications that are actually available outside the United States, but in the United States are being done aftermarket by people who read your sites—essentially creating the ability to extend to the limits of the batteries you already equip a zero emissions mode. They make some significant claims, tens of miles. Would you like to comment on those with your existing product and whether or not that approach, in Toyota's opinion, could be in the future, which would be closer to Dr. Frank's concept?

Mr. HERMANCE. The basic difference between the vehicle as it exists today and Dr. Frank's concept is there is no provision for putting grid electricity, plug-in, into the battery pack. You only have the energy on board within the narrow operating range of the vehicle to use. The actual distance possible with the on-board energy is only about a mile, not tens of miles, in addition to which in the current system without grid replacement of that energy, you have to replace that energy with gasoline, and therefore it is an inefficient operation. In fact, there is an increase in $CO_2$ emission and increase in fuel consumption utilizing that modification of the vehicle as it is currently configured. Some of what they think they are getting, they are not.

Mr. ISSA. Thank you. And I am pleased I was able to get that on the record for my nephew, another Prius owner.

Diane.

Ms. WATSON. Thank you very much. I'm going to direct my questioning to Mr. MacKenzie. He looks like the one that is going to be around with these cars.

Mr. ISSA. Ouch. You could have just said he was your witness, instead of my witnesses are old, and you have the next generation.

Ms. WATSON. I did not say those words, Mr. Chairman. You said "for my son in the future," so I'm calling on someone's son here.

What would you see are the most effective ways to reduce oil consumption in our overall transportation sector?

Mr. MACKENZIE. Well, the No. 1 thing the government can do is to increase fuel economy standards for all vehicles. That's the fastest and most effective, proven way that we have to reduce oil consumption.

Ms. WATSON. Then how can we make sure that the advantages of hybrid penetration are not offset by less fuel-efficient vehicles elsewhere in the fleet? Will hybrid penetration necessarily result in higher fuel economy?

Mr. MACKENZIE. Well, that's a good point. I alluded to that, of course, in my testimony. You see that looking at some of the automakers today, you can see that leading the market in hybrids does not necessarily mean that your fuel economy is going to get better. So promoting hybrids in and of itself is not a guarantee of oil savings. If we want to make progress on our oil dependence, we need to couple those incentives for hybrids with increases in fuel economy standards to ensure that we reap those benefits.

Ms. WATSON. I want to just throw this out, because all of you have been watching what has been going on in the Middle East, and there is a prediction there that all of us would expect that the prices are going to go up. And we are so heavily dependent on oil in the Middle East, and I am just wondering, when will the industry be up to a position where we don't have to be dependent on Middle Eastern oil? You know, the President said we are addicted to oil, and my question is what do all of you feel will be our potential in the manufacturing industry, the high-technology industry, in seeing that all the vehicles that we use are up to a point where we don't depend on foreign oils?

Mr. GERMAN. One of the main problems faced by the auto industry is that the average customer places a relatively low value on fuel economy and fuel savings. If you look at it, you take even $3 a gallon, if you adjust it for the price of inflation and adjust it for the increased efficiency vehicles adjusts compared to what they were in the 1970's, adjust it for the difference in the standards of living and the disposable income, $3 a gallon is still pretty cheap. It is a smaller part of the budget of the average family than fuel was before the first oil crisis in 1973.

Some customers are certainly responding to the increase in gas price. You see that in certain segments, but most customers are not. If you look at it from the standpoint of dollars and cents, it is actually fairly rational.

So this is the problem we face. Society needs reductions in fuel use. Individual customers don't see it as a major part of their purchase decision. There is a disconnect. And it is this disconnect which is the reason why Honda is supporting increases in CAFE standards.

Ms. WATSON. You know, I represent an area in central Los Angeles, and right now the main street in my district is a street called Crenshaw. There is evidence that the youth are coming out at night, and they are doing these donuts. Do you know what a donut is? They go speeding down, and they put their brakes on, and they spin around. It happens after 1 a.m. And I come down that artery and I am saying, my goodness, look at the tracks, look at the gasoline expended.

When you said what you did, Mr. Chairman, I thought we have a tremendous need to educate all our people as to how to make the best use of our resources, gasoline or whatever. The kids have to fill up at the gas station, and in California our gasoline prices have gotten up to $4 from time to time.

Of course, we need better, shall I say, law enforcement, traffic enforcement on our streets. But there is a mentality, it is a lifestyle mentality. Kids do it because that is what you do during this era. So there is a combination of things that we have to grapple with, I think, in our society, because it is really lifestyle, and all of our kids, particularly the gang members, they want to do what everyone else does. It is a real issue as the prices continue to go up and the resources continue to diminish.

Mr. HERMANCE. There are a number of folks in an area not far west of your district that are promoting that with movies like Fast and Furious 1, 2, 3, and several more yet to come, but you're right. There is a huge need for education and a message to be communicated of the value of the resource versus its long-term scarcity. That is not there.

And as John says, right now, if you ask on a list—we survey 31 attributes of a vehicle for purchase decision. Fuel economy used to be dead last. It has moved up, but it is still in the bottom third of reasons for purchase of a specific vehicle, except in very small segments. So you are right, there is a major education process necessary.

Ms. WATSON. Dr. Frank.

Mr. FRANK. Thank you.

Ms. WATSON. I just want to say he is from USC, and that is right in the area that I am talking about. I think you are familiar.

Mr. FRANK. I am at UC Davis.

Mr. ISSA. But he does a wonderful job. Undergraduate Berkeley. Graduate Berkeley. Ph.D. at USC. Now he's at Davis. He covers it all.

Mr. FRANK. Right.

Anyway, the point is the objective is to give the general public, including kids who are doing those donuts, everything they want, but not use gasoline. The real objective is to reduce oil. So the plug-in hybrid which I have been promoting for about 25 years, and I think Dave knows about that, anyway, is one way to do this. The whole objective of the plug-in hybrid is to use electricity, which is equivalent to buying gasoline at 70 cents a gallon. That's the big goal. At 70 cents a gallon people will plug their cars in.

The California Resources Board did not like the idea before, but they do now because the price of gasoline is $3 and $4 a gallon. If you can buy the equivalent power for donuts or whatever, if you buy the equivalent power for 70 cents a gallon, that's the motivation. The question is how do we get the car guys to buy into that?

Ms. WATSON. That's the reason why my question was, Mr. Chairman, is when do you think the industry will be ready to accept that particular option? Car guys?

Mr. HERMANCE. Toyota has announced the intent to pursue the development of a plug-in hybrid. That said, it is probable that it will not be a plug-in hybrid as described by Dr. Frank. The most cost-effective way to use electricity to reduce fuel consumption is not to have all-electric range, but rather to have longer periods that the engine is off during normal operation. That mitigates the need for significantly larger drive motors and power electronics, and this is the evolving direction from the large workshop with DOE of many stakeholders. So it is not necessary that a plug-in vehicle have all-electric range. The benefits are very substantial with much less incremental costs. The incremental costs of large-battery vehicles now is still very high.

Ms. WATSON. You know, there was a statistic that showed that your Honda Accord was the car most often stolen in California. So there is something about that Accord that they love. It has a faster speed? You want to counter that?

Mr. GERMAN. It is just a lot of them are being stolen for parts. You chop it up. We sell 350,000, 400,000 Accords a year. There is a big demand for parts. The latest statistics is the older Accords that are being stolen the most, they are going to chop shops and chopping them up and selling the parts off them.

Ms. WATSON. Thank you, Mr. Chairman.

Mr. ISSA. Thank you. I will try to sum up a few more questions. First of all, I am old enough to remember when the Oldsmobile Cutlass was the most stolen car in America. Now there is no Oldsmobile.

And for those who don't—I think I should confess here, my prior business was the largest manufacturer of car security systems in America. So thank you because Honda made me a Congressman in many ways; however I started the company with Olds Cutlass.

A couple of quick questions. First of all, as we are discussing plug-in hybrids and extended-range batteries for greater amounts—let's just say more electricity, less motor, in a sense aren't we looking for—both of what you are trying to do, we are looking for a sweet spot similar to the one that the train companies found in the 1950's and 1960's and so on. Trains—locomotives that power America have been diesel electric for a very long time for a number of attributes they found: diesels running at constant speed, the advantage of being able to get the amount of power they needed over the drive wheels. And we could go through all the tradeoffs that went into the development of the electric train, which is a universal product basically today.

In a sense, isn't your development—this is primarily for Toyota and Honda—isn't your development to try to find within the market demand for performance and other characteristics the highest overall productive use of the vehicle, both, of course, acceleration, deceleration, fuel economy and emissions? Isn't it sort of a combination that you are working with today, David?

Mr. HERMANCE. Clearly it is. If the buying process were wholly rational, you could tell fuel economy much easier. Since the buying process is often emotional, you have to find the balance of benefits that customers are willing to pay for. That includes fuel economy certainly, but it also includes performance, and at least in California it includes emissions performance. Finding that sweet spot, if you will, the best value proposition is how you get customers to buy your vehicles.

Even if we were to develop independently the best vehicle to solve any specific problem, if we couldn't sell them in significant volume, it wouldn't make any difference. So you have to find something the customers value, they are willing to part with their hard earned money to buy and still reap both societal benefit, and the customer has to feel good about his decision.

Mr. GERMAN. The value proposition is what has led both Toyota and Honda toward small battery packs in primarily assist-type modes. That is because the battery right now is still very expensive, and its energy storage density is very, very small compared to liquid fuel. You are trying to maximize the fuel savings without putting more batteries in, and you have to make sure that the battery is going to last the life of the vehicle, and part of the way we are doing that now is by limiting the change in the energy stakes to very small levels, which greatly improves the life.

Mr. ISSA. We have a little housekeeping before the ranking member is going to have to leave. I would ask unanimous consent that we be able to hold the record open for 2 weeks from this date so that all the Members may make submissions and possible inclusions into the record. Without objection.

I would also ask unanimous consent that this hearing continue until the remainder of this cycle of questions, at which time we will adjourn. Without objection. I thank the ranking member.

That allows us to be very legal in this because this is one of the most bipartisan subcommittees. We have done every one of our hearings in an effort to try to get to the best opportunity for America to go the right direction on energy.

I would like to ask a couple more quick questions. This is not intended to be a speech, but it will sound a little bit like it.

If it is fair to say that the President was right about us being addicted to oil, and that addiction being dangerous, then it would be fair to say that it is, in fact, a national security imperative that we lessen our addiction, slash, dependence on foreign oil.

If that is the case, what messages from Congress within the capabilities of your technology and within the reasonable time constraints to move to those technologies—what messages besides CAFE would best come from Congress that would move the decision process toward lower emissions absolutely—that is certainly something that this Congress is dedicated to—but the higher fuel economy?

I hear all of you, rightfully so, and I spent years selling the products the customer wanted, and every once in a while I would make something that I wanted the customer to want, and very seldom did it end up being what the customer wanted, but Congress has an influence. Used imprudently, we can put your companies into deep, deep recession. We can change the whole nature of the buying pattern. We can cause a recession.

At the same time, what measures do you think would be prudent for Congress to use, besides what we have already talked about, CAFE, to encourage a movement toward dramatically lower fuel consumption, again, within those norms that would allow society not to have a whipsaw?

Mr. HERMANCE. One quick thing I think John mentioned in his testimony and I would reiterate, you could lift the 60,000-unit cap for manufacturers on the hybrid tax credit. We have already gone through the cap. Our customers will cease to realize the full benefit at the end of September. Lifting that cap to allow customers to buy the most efficient vehicles which are the ones that get the largest credit seems a prudent thing to do as a near-term help.

Near term it is hard to do other things immediately. Some longer-term program of education to improve the understanding of the buying public about the value of the scarce commodity is certainly—we have to change buyer behavior somehow so that they value fuel efficiency.

Mr. ISSA. Anyone else?

Mr. FRANK. There are many ways to carry out these benefits. Of course, I have been promoting the use of the plug-in hybrid, and Mr. Chairman mentioned that the cost is high and the batteries and so on. The life is short. We have a lot of evidence that shows that is not quite exactly true.

The Honda—excuse me, the RAV 4, the Toyota RAV 4 electric vehicle batteries are very similar to what we're going to in the plug-in hybrid, I think lasted over 120,000 miles, and Southern California Edison has already shown this, and that is a lifetime battery. The metal hydride batteries have now come down significantly in price over the years. One of the most important things is the plug-in hybrid battery is not the same as the power batteries that are currently used at much lower price per kilowatt hour. There is a lot of evidence to show the battery technology is not so far off. That is No. 1.

No. 2, lithium batteries are much better, much lighter, half the weight for the same amount of energy. So when we go to energy—and Toyota, by the way, has already invested in lithium, and almost everybody else has as well, and all of their competitors are looking at lithium. So the batteries is I don't think as far an issue as before. As I have shown in slides, we can build these cars with long range and not cost anything in weight and incremental costs. I have addressed that. It is much less than you think.

Mr. ISSA. Please.

Mr. GERMAN. I think the primary message from Honda is whatever you do, try to make it performance-based. Don't try to pick specific technologies or whatever. Set out performance standards or incentives and base them on equal footing so manufacturers can develop their own products.

Some States are looking at changes in sales tax based upon the efficiency of the vehicle. You could extend the gas guzzler tax, use those moneys to incorporate more incentives for high-performance vehicles. There are all kinds of possible scenarios out there, including the CAFE. As long as it is performance-based, that is really the key.

Mr. MACKENZIE. In terms of things——

Mr. ISSA. We want to hear from the youth of America, as our ranking member wanted to tell you.

Mr. GERMAN. David, I want to make sure that by performance we don't mean how fast it accelerates. Performance in the efficiency of the consumption of the vehicle.

Mr. ISSA. Both of your companies, for investment in traction control, which the gentlelady was not aware that your traction control vehicles clearly did not leave those marks.

Mr. HERMANCE. There is no switch on our car. You can't shut it off.

Mr. MACKENZIE. I was using performance in the same way, and I want to echo our support for an action that the government could take promptly would be to remove that cap on the number of eligible vehicles for the hybrid tax credit, should be done as soon as possible in the interest of consumers getting a strong and consistent message.

Mr. ISSA. I'm going to ask you a followup question since you are the only one that doesn't have a financial gain if I bring that to fruition. If you were in my seat, would you eliminate the cap on all vehicles, or would you—because it is going to cost money to—at least to the Federal revenue. Would you incentivize that toward the overall higher performing as far as fuel savings vehicles? Would you, in fact, change the existing rules of the road now, or would you simply raise the number?

Mr. MACKENZIE. Well, the structure as it stands is quite good. It is a performance-based system, and those vehicles——

Mr. ISSA. You are happy with the 3,000 and all the different levels?

Mr. MACKENZIE. The levels are fairly reasonable and set up well, so I think the solution is to just remove the cap.

Mr. GERMAN. If I could make one additional comment on that, I am not going to disagree——

Mr. ISSA. He made your case wonderfully. Take "yes" for an answer.

Mr. GERMAN. The current tax incentives are based only on the city fuel economy, and that is not really the best performance metric. Some hybrid systems do better on the city and highway. Diesels do better on the highway. And to make it more neutral, it should be based on the combined fuel economy of the vehicle, not the city. So that would be one positive change that could be made if you are going to change it.

Mr. ISSA. Sure. I am probably overstepping this committee's jurisdiction, but with all due respect to the city and highway measures, I think some of your companies have been lobbying to—I know there has been a small change, but to really modernize the EPA fuel economy standard, to make it as accurate as possible, which it historically has never been. Is that fair to say that is the other part is, yes, make it combined, but also make it—don't make it assume that highway driving is 50 miles an hour, and city driving has this incredibly amount of stops relative to what really happens?

Mr. GERMAN. I won't get into the details because they are monumental, but yes, you are correct.

Mr. MACKENZIE. It is a whole other kettle of fish in a large kettle.

Mr. ISSA. My Committee on Energy and Commerce, which I am on leave of absence from, would assume primary jurisdiction on some of that.

Mr. GERMAN. Just one point. Because of the timeliness requirement, it might be better to quickly lift the cap and then adjust the metric, because the EPA changes in labeling won't occur for at least another year, and the cap is going to be an issue at the end of September.

Mr. ISSA. By the way, I would completely agree with you, except I have seen the history of when we do one and promise to do the other. I am certain that a staggered view all in one bill might, in fact—with a deadline for new standards, might, in fact, be a compromise.

Mr. MacKenzie.

Mr. MACKENZIE. In regards to basing the credits on the combined rather than just the city fuel economy, an additional complication there is that may then be appropriate to adjust what those credit levels are if you are going to adjust your numbers to the combined.

Mr. ISSA. Dr. Frank, because you got your Ph.D. before anyone else in the room, you get the closing statement.

Mr. FRANK. Well, I just want to say that by going to the plug-in hybrid—I will push it one more time—that you get both fuel economy in city and highway because of the downsized gasoline engine. All the performance comes from the electric motor. So I have to disagree with Mr. German from Honda a little bit. Toyota certainly knows that they have done a very good job, but when you go to the plug-in hybrid, everything gets better. You can downsize the engine much further and get city and highway fuel economy both.

Mr. ISSA. I thank you all for your testimony. I would be remiss if I didn't make a plug that if California lifts its ban on nuclear energy, and as a result we are using far less fossil fuel to produce our electricity, although the 70 cents may still be 70 cents, the emissions benefit goes to a zero emissions.

With that, I will make my closing remarks. From what I have heard here today—and, by the way, we really did look at your statements before I made "what I heard here today"—it is clear that the breakthroughs in technology and manufacturing are needed to improve hybrid cars. It is also clear that those are on the horizon. We can increase their efficiency and commercialize plug-in hybrids to reduce the Nation's reliance on unstable foreign suppliers of oil.

The hybrid car market is not a niche market in America, and manufacturers must acknowledge this fact. Consumers are clamoring for more hybrids, and today, with the increased CAFE standards, the next generation of hybrids can provide a foundation for reducing U.S. petroleum consumption.

I'd like to thank our witnesses here today for such an informative hearing. And once again, there is no level of thanks this committee can give for people who come together from very different backgrounds, from academia, from, to be honest, the for-profit car companies, and from think tanks and bring together just consistency that the direction that we are going is just the beginning; the direction that we can go is up to you, but it is also up to Congress. With that, I hope this record will help the rest of the Congress seek some of these solutions. We stand adjourned.

[Whereupon, at 4:03 p.m., the subcommittee was adjourned.]

○

CPSIA information can be obtained at www.ICGtesting.com
Printed in the USA
BVOW08s1550161213

339281BV00011B/778/P